Nigel Rooms is Director of Min
Diocese of Southwell and N
Bestwood Park with Rise Park
Christchurch Cathedral in th
Tanzania. He worked as a Mission Partner in Tanzania from
1994 until 2001, developing an innovative Theological Education
by Extension course in Swahili, running an international
congregation and building a new church. He holds an MA in
Mission and Ministry from Nottingham University and a ThD
in Missiology from Birmingham University, and has research
and other interests in contextual theology, adult theological
education, leadership and ministerial formation and emerging
church. He is the editor of the *Journal of Adult Theological
Education* published by Equinox. He is married to Karen, also
a priest, and they have two teenage sons. They live in inner-city
Nottingham where he enjoys working on his allotment and
agonizing over the fluctuating fortunes of his beloved 'Tigers' –
Hull City AFC.

THE FAITH OF THE ENGLISH

Integrating Christ and culture

Nigel Rooms

First published in Great Britain in 2011

Society for Promoting Christian Knowledge
36 Causton Street
London SW1P 4ST
www.spckpublishing.co.uk

Copyright © Nigel Rooms 2011

All rights reserved. No part of this book may be reproduced or transmitted in any form or by any means, electronic or mechanical, including photocopying, recording, or by any information storage and retrieval system, without permission in writing from the publisher.

SPCK does not necessarily endorse the individual views contained in its publications.

The author and publisher have made every effort to ensure that the external website and email addresses included in this book are correct and up to date at the time of going to press. The author and publisher are not responsible for the content, quality or continuing accessibility of the sites.

Unless otherwise noted, Scripture quotations are translated by the author.
Quotations marked 'CEV' are taken from the *Contemporary English Version* New Testament © American Bible Society 1991, 1992, 1995; Anglicizations copyright The British and Foreign Bible Society 1995. Used with permission. For more information about the Contemporary English Version, please visit <www.bibleresources.org.uk>.
Quotations marked 'KJV' are from the Authorized Version of the Bible (The King James Bible), the rights in which are vested in the Crown, and are reproduced by permission of the Crown's Patentee, Cambridge University Press.
Quotations marked 'NIV' are taken from the HOLY BIBLE, NEW INTERNATIONAL VERSION. Copyright © 1973, 1978, 1984 by International Bible Society. Used by permission of Hodder & Stoughton Publishers, a member of the Hachette UK Group. All rights reserved. 'NIV' is a registered trademark of International Bible Society. UK trademark number 1448790.
Quotations marked 'REB' are taken from the Revised English Bible, copyright © Oxford University Press and Cambridge University Press 1989.
Quotations marked 'RSV' are from the Revised Standard Version of the Bible, copyright © 1946, 1952 and 1971 by the Division of Christian Education of the National Council of the Churches of Christ in the USA. Used by permission. All rights reserved.
Extracts from The Book of Common Prayer, the rights in which are vested in the Crown, are reproduced by permission of the Crown's Patentee, Cambridge University Press.

British Library Cataloguing-in-Publication Data
A catalogue record for this book is available from the British Library

ISBN 978–0–281–06111–2

1 3 5 7 9 10 8 6 4 2

Typeset by Graphicraft Ltd, Hong Kong
Printed in Great Britain by MPG Books Group

Produced on paper from sustainable forests

I would like to dedicate this book in memory of my grandparents, Nora and Reg Soar, who unwittingly and in very different ways rooted me in home and place

'The Word became flesh; he made his home among us,
and we saw his glory . . . full of grace and truth'

The Gospel of John (REB)

'And did those feet in ancient time
walk upon England's mountains green?'

William Blake

Contents

Introduction

A story is told of the days of apartheid in South Africa when the white English Fathers of the Community of the Resurrection worked in a black township outside Johannesburg. No one is quite sure whether it concerns the more famous Trevor Huddleston or one of his contemporaries, but for our purposes it doesn't really matter – the story is about a white English priest (Allen, 2006, p. 26). Every day the priest had to walk from home to the church to say Mass and every day he passed the house of a woman who took in washing to make her meagre living. Most days she would be pegging out clothes on the line in the African sun as the priest made his way along the road by her house. It being Africa and the priest being white, he naturally had a big black hat and a flowing white cassock to protect him from that sun. And every time he passed the woman at her work with the washing he would doff his hat to her. A normal and everyday sign of respect and even reverence in English culture, a thing he probably didn't even notice he was doing. One day the woman's teenage son was present and noticed this event, and was shocked to his core that a white man would show respect to a poor black woman in the days of apartheid. It moved him and he never forgot it – especially since he too, in time, joined the ranks of the Community of the Resurrection as a priest. His name was and still is Desmond.

This is a story of ordinary English courtesy and politeness in the service of the gospel. The gospel that proclaims the good news to everyone regardless of their colour. It is a story I wanted to begin this book with because it signposts what we shall be exploring throughout the forthcoming chapters.

The story illustrates the 'hiddenness' of culture to those within it. We do not notice our own culture because we are brought up simply to assume it – it slips under the surface of our lives in our early years to do its hidden work. So, in order to see what drives us, we shall want to find ways of digging down into behaviour like the doffing of a hat. The story shows us that our culture only really becomes visible when placed alongside another culture, and the question that raises, for those of us who do not live and work outside England, is: how can we become more aware of our own culture if it is so hidden down below? We cannot start any kind of integration with our faith if we don't recognize our culture when it manifests itself.

The question of faith is therefore raised – it mattered in the story that the priest was a man of faith on his way to his daily devotion. There seems to be a natural, self-deprecating, un-hurried beauty about his behaviour that might only come from a Christian Englishman. As the title of this book suggests, there-fore, there could be a real and deep connection between the kind of hidden English culture that we naturally and unconsciously display and the Christian faith which has been part of our national life for over 1,500 years. But is this right? We know that not all the things that white English missionaries did in their work in the 'colonies' served the gospel in quite the same way as the priest in our story. Indeed, getting excited about being English has been more associated with right-wing racist groups in recent years. So we are going to put English culture and the Christian faith into dialogue such that we hope both might emerge transformed. Our aim will be to see if there is a proper, good and true integration of English culture and the Christian faith to be found, and if so, what it might look like.

Finally, our priest was on a journey in mission each day from home to church. Yet today you are unlikely to notice the doffing of a hat as a sign of politeness. So, on the journey that we'll be sharing together, I hope you'll find yourself asking questions about mission in contemporary England beyond the days when Christendom could be assumed and God might be thought of as an Englishman (see Moreton, 2010).

At this point it is worth outlining the shape of the book, the journey that we are going to make and some of the things we might need to be aware of on the way.

This book is presented first and foremost as a work of theology, but as the reader will find out, the emphasis is on what is known these days as practical theology and in some ways could be also termed missiology – theological reflection on the missionary task of sharing the gospel of Jesus Christ. As is necessary in practical theology, we'll be dipping into other disciplines on the journey – most notably social anthropology and theories of learning and adult theological education.

Perhaps here we need a kind of health warning, as I hope the previous paragraph doesn't put you off. For some people might get as far as the word theology and think this book is not for them. What I want to say here is that I have written the book for those readers who are often described as 'thinking Christians', a term that is quite inadequate because much of the book could just as easily be read by people who don't consider themselves Christians – and really, are there such people as 'unthinking Christians'? The book does therefore require some level of engagement with theological ideas, but I have tried wherever concepts need to be introduced to explain them fully and give examples. Overall I have written the book holding especially in mind all those who would count England as home, but who are also restless about what is beyond its horizon.

While the book stands alone as a work of practical theology, I am also offering with it a short theological adult learning course which I hope will fulfil the aim, expressed in the book as a whole, of integrating Christian faith and English culture. The course is designed for anyone (although those wanting to facilitate it would benefit from some level of adult education skills) who would like to think about the relationship between Englishness and the Christian faith in a small group learning environment. Thus part of the journey in the book is explaining how this course came to be created, what the thinking behind it is and what results have been discovered so far when running it.

I begin in Chapter 1 by introducing our first concept – that of inculturation. Here we are firmly in the field of missiology and its reflection during the past 40 or so years on the relationship between faith and culture around the world – the very stuff we want to explore. We'll also begin to understand at the end of that chapter the relationship between missiology, practical theology and adult theological learning.

Chapter 2 attempts to describe Englishness and looks at the burgeoning literature on the subject over the past few years. Several approaches to understanding Englishness are explored, including that of investigating our historical and sometimes mythical origins. We conclude the chapter with a comprehensive description of the 'cultural heart' of the English from the social anthropologist Kate Fox (2004).

We pick up the theme of learning most fully in Chapter 3, where the theory and method behind the course that goes along with the book is fully explained. It is perhaps the most complex of all the chapters as it requires a discussion of hermeneutics – the theory and practice of interpreting texts or finding meaning in them. While it isn't absolutely necessary for the argument of the whole book, I hope most readers will stay with it – not least because I argue for the importance of using the imagination in our theology and mission today, a much neglected area.

In Chapter 4, we take a side road into the greenwood! This chapter, focusing as it does on the Robin Hood legends, stands alone as a theological reflection in its own right. It is important in the book, though, as it provides an example of the kind of work that needs to be done if there is to be such a thing as an emergent English contextual theology. It is a contribution to the *deep listening* to our culture that I believe is necessary.

I am not the only writer of this book. Chapter 5 distils the work of several small groups of willing participants (to whom I am very grateful) who piloted the Englishness course for me. This is where we begin that integration, conversation and dialogue between the description of Englishness we discovered in Chapter 2 and the gospel as we have received it. I present the initial findings there, but they are only initial because, I hope, as the course is run again and again new insights should continue to emerge.

The book concludes with a slightly more speculative chapter wondering about the implications of English inculturation for mission today in our land. In these last two chapters I hope to pose more questions than answers to the reader, not least because that is the kind of time we are in. My desire is that as you interact with the questions you might be stimulated to go on thinking and working with the issues raised.

Before we finally get going I would like to say thanks for reading the book. If you have any questions, or you would like some advice on running your own version of the Englishness course, do not hesitate to get in touch with me. I always respond to emails sent to <nigel.rooms@southwell.anglican.org>.

1

Inculturation – or integrating faith and culture

I have only once, in 40 or so years as a Christian, been led in worship in my own 'vernacular'. My first language is English, but there are a huge variety of local variations of it, as we all know, and I grew up speaking one of them – my 'vernacular'.

It happened a few years ago. I was attending a service at a local theological college, at which the ministers leading the worship were a couple in training from my home town of Hull. The English accent native to the East Riding of Yorkshire is a particular and peculiar one and I grew up with it for the first 18 years of my life. I have not lived there permanently since, but the experience of being transported there via the familiar words of the liturgy was extraordinary. Somehow heaven and earth (or rather 'airth', to use my vernacular!) were connected now in a new and exciting way.

I finally had a personal experience of what I had observed among the Tanzanian Christians alongside whom I worked for seven years in the 1990s. Although our Anglican worship was conducted in the Tanzanian national language, Kiswahili, the words of the liturgy and the hymns were normally translated from English equivalents. Use of Kiswahili in worship was right and good, since it has united over 120 tribes with different languages into a Tanzanian nation with a distinct identity – but it still meant that many people were worshipping God in their second, not their first language. Kiswahili often wasn't their true 'vernacular'. But just occasionally a hymn or chorus would be sung to the local musical idiom of a particular tribe or even in a vernacular language itself. The joy and vibrancy and the holistic sense of the singers' involvement in the event was in stark contrast to how hymns were normally sung, stiffly and with some distance. Underneath the joy was also a longing, a questioning, even a resistance, giving silent voice to the problem of why this didn't happen more often. 'Why can't my faith and my culture be more integrated?' was the unspoken question that seemed to lie just under the surface.

I was in Tanzania at the invitation of the Anglican Church to develop a 'Theological Education by Extension' (TEE) programme. TEE is like open learning in the UK, in that studies take place part-time at home with written materials as the 'teacher' rather than in an expensive residential college. Asked to write a short course of studies in Kiswahili for lay Christians at the 'grass roots' on, literally, the 'spiritual life', I could not avoid the issue I have just explained. To put it somewhat crudely, how can individuals and the community be both authentically African and authentically Christian? The question is made sharper because the Christianity Africans have inherited is not African in origin but European. After several generations some African culture may already have been lost because of European Christianity's influence. African Christians end up then in the difficult position of having one foot in their (somewhat neutered) African culture and one foot in European Christianity (which doesn't sit happily with them). To put the question another way: is there a more solid foundation on which they can stand in an authentic *African Christianity* that takes both their indigenous culture and the new-found faith seriously?

The question I was addressing is that of 'inculturation', a term theologians and missiologists have coined in the past few decades; simply put, it considers *the proper relationship between faith and culture.*

I returned to work in England early in the twenty-first century, continuing in adult theological education and training in the Anglican Church. The questions my African experience had raised stayed with me and I decided to look into them in more depth.

I soon discovered, though, that the situation as regards questions of faith and culture in the 'post-modern' West, and particularly in England, is not entirely unrelated to the African one. As many people have pointed out in the last decade or so, the Church here as an institution often looks back to a time when it was much more 'of' the culture, to borrow a phrase from Niebuhr's *Christ and Culture* (1951). This is the 'Christendom' mode of church, where assumptions about the proximity and overlap of church and state, culture and faith could be made.

So English Christians, it seems, inherit an assumption that was much more prevalent in previous generations, but nevertheless still lingers on – that to be English is somehow synonymous with being Christian. At the 2001 census, and depending somewhat on the region of the country, around 70 per cent of people still claimed to be adherents of the Christian faith. Opinion differs widely among both Christian commentators and secular sociologists of religion as to what most of them meant by this or what the implications of the claim might be for the Church and its mission, yet clearly we are still able to some extent to call ourselves a 'Christian' country.

England has been some kind of a Christian country for more than one thousand years, so we might expect many aspects of our culture to have been influenced by the majority faith (Spencer, 2010). What I am interested in exploring in this book is the relationship between inherited English culture and Christian faith (we shall return to the question of the decline of Christendom and its implications for mission in the final chapter). Foundational to the work of the book, therefore, is a proper understanding of the idea of inculturation, and it is to that task that I now turn.[1]

In examining the term 'inculturation', we will review what has been written on the subject, look at the derivation of the word itself and scrutinize the concept theologically. We will attempt a particular definition, distilled from this work, that will

---

[1] This chapter is based on, but also much modified and developed from, a journal article I wrote some years ago (Rooms, 2005).

be useful for us. Such a definition will require further examination and clarification of the meaning of the 'Christian faith' or 'gospel' as well as culture itself. The question of 'why' inculturation is so important will be explored alongside examining approaches to its process, the 'how', and its content, the 'what'. The limits of inculturation and a critique of it will be generated alongside a discussion of its usefulness for theology, education and learning in the Church.

What is inculturation? – a definition

A good starting point for thinking about inculturation is to ask a basic question, such as: how has Christianity expanded throughout the centuries? The missiologist Andrew Walls (1999) suggests imagining how an interplanetary scholar of religion with a long life and a periodic research grant might address the vastly different forms of Christianity she (or it?) finds when a field study is made every few centuries. What would the connection be between a small Jewish sect following the teachings of Jesus in the first century and Irish monks doing penance by saying prayers while standing up to their waists in the freezing sea? What do the arguments around the Greek word *homoousios* at the Council of Nicea in the fourth century have to do with sending missionaries to Africa in the nineteenth? Can we discern any continuity between these versions of Christianity? Walls thinks we can, and more of that later.

In a further work Walls compares the expansion of Christianity and Islam. He claims that Christianity's story is one of advance and regression in comparison with the steady geographical progression of Islam (2002, p. 13):

> When it comes to sustaining congregations of the faithful, Christianity does not appear to possess the same resilience as Islam. It decays and withers in its very heartlands, in the areas where it appears to have had the profoundest cultural effects. Crossing cultural boundaries, it then takes root anew on the margins of those areas, and beyond. Islamic expansion is progressive; Christian expansion is serial.

Walls claims this is because Christianity has no culturally fixed element, like the Qur'an, being based as it is on the *person* of Jesus Christ. The unchangeable, even untranslatable Word of the Qur'an and Islam is starkly contrasted with the eternal, pre-existing, personal Word of John's Gospel (John 1.1). So, using the theological idea of incarnation (which we will see is key to understanding inculturation), where the 'Word' ceases to be made flesh (John 1.14) within a community, then 'that community is likely to lose not just its effectiveness, but its powers of resistance'. It is the 'sustained, unceasing penetration of the host culture' (2002, p. 13) that maintains the faith within that culture.

So we know that the thriving Christian communities that once existed throughout the Roman period in what is today Turkey and North Africa no longer survive. Walls claims one very important reason for this was that they ceased to relate the Christian faith to the culture around them by incarnating Christ to others – and it followed that the Church essentially 'died' in these areas. The interaction of Christian faith and culture is then literally a 'matter of life and death' and is the raw material for the study of inculturation.

Inculturation is a 'neologism', that is, a word never in use before which has been 'invented' by Christian theologians working in the field of faith and culture in the last 40 or so years. Some authors think that the word was developed to bring together the sociological term ac*culturation* (see further below) and the theological term *in*carnation. As we shall see, it is important not to mix up the word with another sociological term, *enculturation* – this is something subtly different.

The metaphor of a battery may help us here. Inculturation happens in the interaction between the two 'poles' of faith and culture – like the positive and negative terminals of a battery. What can look like very different entities (and which are often kept apart theologically by many in our churches) come together to produce energy, creativity and newness – and even a few sparks from time to time!

Roman Catholic theologians have generally used the term inculturation since just before, and then during and after the

Second Vatican Council in the 1960s. Protestants on the other hand have tended not to employ the word until more recently, preferring the word 'contextualization'. Inculturation as an acceptable term for Protestants, however, is becoming more popular, especially after it was used widely in the report *Mission-shaped Church* in 2004. Contextualization is perhaps a more flexible term, one which is often utilized to widen the meaning of the second pole of culture to anything that has to do with the context in which Christian faith is set (e.g. political and economic contexts). Although we will touch on these in this book, we are more concerned with culture itself (and we'll look at definitions of culture in a moment), so we'll stay with inculturation rather than contextualization.

How then can inculturation be defined? One helpful approach is to start from a sociological perspective and understand the term as a new theological idea that is to be found in the space between the sociological terms 'enculturation' and 'acculturation'.

Enculturation is socialization – a process that can be seen in children who are brought up within a culture to observe and obey its cultural and social norms. The person finds himself or herself as *of* the culture when the process is complete. What happens is that the culture is taken for granted – it becomes 'normal' and assumptions can be made about how to act and behave within that culture. This is why it is difficult to cross cultures, because when we attempt to do so the assumptions that are made are often subtly different. A few years ago we went as a family to America (even more tricky in some ways than going somewhere 'really foreign', as they speak – sort of – the same language). We wanted to send home some postcards so we went to the post office to buy some stamps – only to be looked at with incredulity, because obviously stamps aren't sold in post offices but in supermarkets (doh!).

Acculturation, meanwhile, is the process of two cultures meeting over an extended period of time, by which both cultures are changed. We now know that chicken tikka masala is one of the most popular dishes in the UK – it currently beats hands down old-fashioned meat and two veg or even fish and chips.

Of course it isn't authentically Indian, but a fusion of something between the tastes of India and England, and thus it illustrates the idea of acculturation very well. However, acculturation is often governed by power relations, in that the more powerful culture determines the path of cultural change. So the African-Caribbean people who arrived in this country in large numbers from the 1950s onwards found it very difficult to worship in Anglican churches for lots of reasons, not least of which was that any acculturation was expected to happen almost wholly on the part of the newcomers. However, when acculturation does occur, cultural change will always be the outcome. It is impossible then to move outside the bounds of one particular culture without being changed culturally and bringing into existence a new cultural state.

So, having understood these two ideas, it is possible to 'translate' the terms enculturation and acculturation from sociology into theology. Enculturation can be likened to the incarnation – Christ as the Word takes on full humanity in becoming one of us and dwelling among us (John 1.14) – but this leads, it seems inevitably, through Jesus' inauguration of the kingdom of God (an alternative 'world') to the cross where his mortal life is transformed through his death and resurrection. This latter movement, it seems to me, is analogous to the process of acculturation.

The same movement can be applied to our understanding of culture. Incarnation, in this analogical sense, is then the enculturation of the Word, the gospel or the Christian faith within a culture such that it becomes *of* it and identified with it. The process of enculturation is not, however, all there is to the relationship of Christ and culture. As we have just noted, Christ was crucified as a result of his very incarnation and raised from death to 'convert' or transform both humanity and human culture. Thus there is a converting acculturation implied by the prior enculturation whereby the host culture is not only indwelt by Christian faith but converted and transformed by it. Timothy Gorringe also uses the analogy of the cross and resurrection for the acculturation effect and quotes Aylward

Shorter's approach to culture: 'Cultures are to be evangelized and challenged to *metanoia*, to die to all that is not worthy of humanity in their traditions, but then to rise in greater splendour' (2004, p. 100).

Perhaps another analogy might help our understanding here. Think about the process of eating, which is essential for life and growth among all living things. The food first has to be assimilated into the body – it has to become *one* with it, by whatever process of digestion is available. But in the very act of assimilating, the body is changed irrevocably by the presence of the nutrients within it. It has to accommodate to them. So it is with our faith – it has to live within a culture and cannot really exist apart from culture, but by its very presence in that culture it has a transforming effect. Incidentally, this analogy is also perhaps one of the reasons why it is so important for Christians to physically eat the bread and drink the wine at the Eucharist.

Therefore the importance of the incarnation for a theology of culture cannot be underestimated (Gorringe, 2004; Magesa, 2004). We must be careful though, as I have already hinted, not to collapse the idea of inculturation into that of pure enculturation – that it is just about becoming part of or identified with a culture. We must hold together these two different ideas – of incarnation and conversion/transformation – in the theological term inculturation.

It follows that inculturation is both at first a movement into the culture and then a transformational movement which creates something new. It is what we could call a 'double movement' of incarnation and conversion, to use theological words. Perhaps the most helpful understanding of inculturation in this mode is again from Andrew Walls (1999), in which he proposes the 'indigenizing' principle of incarnation and the 'pilgrim' principle of transformation and change.

We can now define inculturation as a process that can be discovered in the creative tension between culture and faith, enculturation and acculturation, incarnation and conversion. Since culture, like the Church, is always in *process* (Gorringe, 2004), inculturation is dynamic not static, which means that it is always ongoing and necessarily incomplete. So it becomes part of what it means to live 'between the times' – between Christ's first coming in the flesh and his second coming, which will be very different and yet will inaugurate that age when all cultures (literally ethnicities) are represented in heaven (Rev. 5.9). This book then is about inculturation among the English – or trying to understand the ongoing and ever-changing dynamic of the relationship between English culture and the Christian faith.

The importance of process is a vital point to understand, since there are those (including some who criticize strongly the work of missionaries) who would like to 'freeze' cultures in time and not allow the very natural processes of change to occur. An example is the iconic Masai (usually men) of East Africa, much loved of Land-Rover advertisements a few years ago and of the BBC, who used their dancing to introduce programmes. Masai men wear as standard dress a red tartan-like blanket tied around their body (from some angles the garment is quite revealing) and because this looks nothing like Western clothes it is easy to assume that they have always dressed this way; it is an appealing aspect of their 'traditional' culture. This is until one realizes that before woollen mills were introduced into Kenya as late as the 1920s the Masai wore red-dyed animal skins. I once even noted a Masai boy in higher education in a town who had converted his blanket into a shirt and shorts – the start of a new trend? Culture is always changing, and inculturation is about changing it in an authentically Christian direction.

Having arrived at a working definition of inculturation, and before moving on to examine the 'why,' 'how' and 'what' that underlie it, I want now to define further the two 'poles' of the inculturation battery.

The pole of Christian faith – or 'gospel'

In the last section I made the claim that the Christian faith does not really exist apart from culture. This claim, however, needs justifying, as there are many who would want to say that there is some core element(s) to what we call 'the gospel' which can be isolated and applied to any context or culture. This approach implies that becoming Christian means assenting to these core truths and then trying consistently to apply them to our lives. But what if we, as the English, are much more mixed up than that, especially after over a thousand years of Christian history? Perhaps we can't separate our faith and culture so easily.

The issues at stake here are very important; the Christian faith has been and still is practised as a missionary faith with a *universal* claim on the whole of the world in every culture, but can its universality be isolated? Is there a 'core' gospel which can be 'distilled' and applied in any context? We thought in the Victorian era we were exporting a universal gospel, but we have since discovered how much of that version of Christianity was tied up with culture (and, to some extent, imperialism). On the other hand, if there is nothing that can give us a universal element in our faith, how can we recognize different cultural variations of Christianity around the world? And how then can there be any authentic inculturation?

It is easy to think that the actual practice of the Christian Church throughout the centuries has assumed a 'core' gospel, otherwise how would we know what was an authentic expression of faith? But such a view does not fully take into account the political realities of the relationship of church and power after the Roman Empire became Christianized in the fourth century.

In any case, even if there were a 'core' gospel, what exactly would its content be? We could assume rather loosely that a gospel exists without defining its content, or we could try and define it as perhaps the whole of the 'Judaeo-Christian tradition'. Gerald Arbuckle (1990), a Roman Catholic, has a very broad definition bringing together gospel, kingdom of heaven and word of God under the metaphor of a seed being sown in the soil of culture. Yet then he adds to it the tradition, or the 'doctrine, teaching and practice of the Church', of which the

Scriptures are only a part. This is complex! However, for many Protestants perhaps the gospel simply means the Scriptures, with some wanting to add the Creeds.

The issue here, as I have already hinted, is that we as Christians are looking for a universal factor that will enable the global integrity (or catholicity, to use the theological term) of the Christian faith to be maintained. I don't think that we can use the image of a 'gospel' kernel that can be isolated from a cultural husk any more. No, the gospel does not exist apart from a cultural domain (Magesa, 2004) – perhaps as a heart cannot beat without a body or a fish cannot breathe without water. However, neither do I think that the best metaphor is that of the onion, which has been used from time to time as an illustration in opposition to the kernel idea. In an onion each layer may be peeled off, but there is no kernel that is different from the rest, that is, there is no isolatable gospel – there is no universal element. In the end the gospel and its cultural domain are in some kind of dynamic *relationship* which does not lend itself to the static images of seeds and onions.

In our world today we find it difficult to think that there are universals that apply to every human person – that there is one story to which everyone can relate. We suspect such universals because of our history and the threat of being colonized by them and the perceived reduction in choice that might ensue. However, most anthropologists, who study culture and human behaviour at its most basic level, recognize what they call 'cross-cultural universals', even if they cannot agree entirely on what they might be (Fox, 2004).

Gorringe (2004) argues from philosophy and sociology for a shared universal humanity, and the idea that there are universal human rights must also be related to this. In relation to our faith he states (2004, pp. 220–1) that the Christian claim to universal salvation is rooted in the incarnation, where the particular taking up of a life in a place and time becomes of universal significance – it is not therefore what he has termed a 'false universal' (such as colonizing empires and the forces of globalization):

the task [of the Christian movement] ... is to live out and witness to the breaking down of all barriers.... it is a vision of a *process*. The true universal ... is an endless struggle and true universalists are not those who preach global tolerance but those who engage in a passionate fight for the Truth which enthuses them.

So this gives us a clue to solving our problem – rather than some static *thing*, we are looking for a *process* that can be the universal element joining faith and culture together.

Walls concludes his discussion of the question of the essential continuity in the different epochs of Christianity referred to at the beginning of the chapter by stating that despite the vast differences in outward forms there *is* a discernible essential continuity of different processes: 'continuity of thought about the final significance of Jesus, continuity of a certain consciousness about history, continuity in the use of the Scriptures, of bread and wine, of water' (1999, p. 21).

Kwame Bediako (1999) develops Walls' work and names the process operating here as 'translation'. He does not mean translation in the literal sense of transferring the meaning of words between different languages; rather that the Christian religion is 'culturally infinitely translatable'. He wants to say that the universal element in the Christian faith is the very fact that it has a proper continuity in *any* culture. So there is no place which may not, because of the prevailing culture, be ready and able to receive the good news. Translatability is then understood as universality, such that the Christian faith has a 'fundamental relevance and accessibility to persons in any culture'.

This approach turns upside-down the usual movement we noted above in inculturation from the seed of faith being inserted into culture. Rather, in dynamic interaction between faith and culture an inculturated 'gospel' emerges which is a 'new thing' peculiar to that culture and context. Bediako calls this phenomenon 'indigeneity'; 'translatability is the only true basis and starting point for seeking indigeneity'. Translatability is therefore assumed to be an integral part of the gospel and the Christian faith and its universal characteristic. Bediako concludes (1999, p. 156): 'thus universality, translatability, incarnation and indigeneity belong in a continuum and are integral to the warp and woof of the Christian religion'.

Gorringe concurs on the wider human scale: 'Cultural *difference* is not the same as cultural *untranslatability* and it is not clear that, if it was, notions of the human *species* could have arisen' (2004, his emphasis).

We are now in a position to answer the questions posed at the beginning of this section. Translatability holds together both the universal and the particular elements of our faith in a helpful way – we can be both truly global and local with this understanding. It also seems to avoid the tendency to colonizing or 'false universals' that we have sometimes been guilty of in the history of our faith. And we have learnt it from an African theologian working alongside a British missiologist! Translatability offers the Church a way of doing mission whereby the missioner or evangelist can be simultaneously 'missioned' or evangelized.

A good example of this is the encounter between Peter and Cornelius in the Acts of the Apostles. We are presented with the story twice (Acts 10 and 11.1–18) which, given Luke has limited space in which to explain the initial expansion of the gospel, is remarkable. The question is, who is actually being converted in this narrative? Cornelius, it seems, only needs to understand about Jesus Christ and then receive the Holy Spirit, whereas Peter has a deep and long journey to make against his own prejudices.

Lamin Sanneh, another African theologian now working in the United States, also addresses the same questions: 'Thus if we ask the question about the essence of Christianity, whatever the final answer, we would be forced to reckon with what the fresh medium reveals to us in feedback' (1999, p. 53). What he means is that when a culture encounters Christian faith, a 'fresh medium' is created which feeds back something new to us to add to the sum total of what historical and global Christianity is.

Thus while the 'gospel', the essence or message of the faith, may not have an existence separate from culture, nevertheless there is a recognizable continuity or 'rootedness' in the tradition. The implication of this 'feedback' is that whenever authentic mission takes place with the aim of inculturation there will be what Clemens Sedmak (2002) calls a 'reappropriation' of the tradition or 'gospel'.

Such reappropriation is the practical outcome of Fr Vincent Donovan's work among the East African Masai, as described in his classic book *Christianity Rediscovered* (1978). This text is now widely used in Western countries as a working example of what we have been theorizing about – as it was in *Mission-shaped Church* (2004) – and is well worth reading. Whatever the long term-effects of Donovan's work,[2] it helps us to see the faith and culture question more starkly, simply because the Masai culture is so vastly different from our own. We can then start making the connections closer to home.

The pole of culture

If only we could come up with one definition of 'culture'! Like 'spirituality' and 'ministry' it has a range of meanings, and there seem to be as many definitions as authors who write about it. In fact culture is a whole field of study in itself, and since the mid-nineteenth century there have been a progression of approaches to it, using a mixture of philosophy, political theory, sociology and anthropology.

Gorringe (2004) is clear that culture is of 'fundamental theological concern'. We have already seen how he stresses the importance of process in culture and therefore social change. Thus for him culture is 'the name of that whole process in the course of which God does what it takes . . . to make and to keep human beings human. Culture in this sense is, under God, "the human task"' (2004, p. 4).

Any approach to culture that takes a static view of it will not be helpful. This is one of Gorringe's several objections, following the American Mennonite John Yoder, to Richard Niebuhr's classic work *Christ and Culture* (1951), which I have already

---

[2] Some rather negative evidence has recently emerged – see Bowen, John P., '"What happened next?" Vincent Donovan Thirty-five years on', *International Bulletin of Missionary Research*, Vol. 33, No. 2, April 2009.

referred to. Here Niebuhr suggested that Christ (meaning the Church and Christians in general) could be variously against, of or above culture, among other positions. But Gorringe is clear that any person or community could at one and the same time take any or all of Niebuhr's positions (or typologies) to the culture they find themselves in because of its fluid nature.

From a missiological perspective Robert Schreiter offers another approach to culture in his major work *Constructing Local Theologies* (1985). Schreiter asserts that a relevant theory of culture will need to address itself to holism (that is, all aspects of a local culture, not just the 'high' or interesting ones; football and bingo as well as polo and opera), identity and social change. Having reviewed several different approaches to culture and found these wanting, Schreiter opts for a 'semiotic' (anthropological) approach based on the work of Clifford Geertz. Semiotics interprets the signs and symbols presented by a culture (things like black cats, the raising of two fingers in a 'v' backwards or forwards, wearing white at a wedding and black at a funeral, etc.).

We cannot here go into a lengthy analysis of Schreiter's work, but it can be said that his deployment of semiotics is one widely taken up by actual practitioners. The study of semiotics is a highly skilled and academic field which is beyond the scope of this book. However, proverbs, sayings and metaphors have been used to describe a culture comprehensively both in Africa and the United States (Healey and Sybertz, 1997; Nussbaum, 1998). And as we shall see in Chapter 2, Kate Fox in her book *Watching the English* (Fox, 2004) has made an approach to English culture through popular sayings and proverbs that arises from a prior anthropological and semiotic study of the English. We will not need to worry too much about how Fox reaches her conclusions, rather we will want to understand how we might use key sayings and proverbs which encapsulate English culture.

We can place alongside this semiotic approach the work of Gorringe (2004), who proposes three theological themes or elements that help us to understand and define culture. Interestingly these overlap with what we have already learnt about inculturation – that it occurs between the 'indigenizing' and the 'pilgrim' and is a process.

So he begins with the incarnation and the Word becoming 'flesh' and offers the following definition: '"Flesh", as John spells out in some detail in the course of his meditations, means culture – food, the world of symbols, the way in which we cherish bodies' (2004, p. 18). For Gorringe, then, culture is a wider field than just semiotics, including the very basic needs of humans, such as food, and going right through to politics and economics. We should note here how culture works itself out in a physical way – the inculturation of the English will have implications for what we do with and where we put our very bodies.

Second, says Gorringe, the gospel meets every culture with 'sharp scepticism'. No culture entirely embodies the kingdom, while 'antagonism and alienation' often exist at the heart of culture. The imperial history of the Church, the colonial period, the Holocaust – 'the dark side of cultural history' – all have to be faced. Scepticism is never the last word, however, because of the fact of the incarnation. Culture at its best can be revelatory, which gives it a 'sacramental or signifying role'. This leaves us with something fundamental about culture, which is that it refers to meaning and value. The meaning a person places on the world, the values he or she holds and the actions that ensue all constitute that person's culture. Again we would expect that if English Christians are to attempt an integration of their faith and culture this will affect the meaning they place on life and their values.

Finally Gorringe returns to the theme mentioned above, of process and change in culture. This is the eschatological dimension – the process 'of becoming'. Therefore culture is always an unfinished process, which implies that any partial end or 'state' of inculturation is not necessarily recognizable from the beginning – inculturation cannot be prescriptive (Gittins, 1993). We are, as has been noted, on a journey here.

Perhaps overall then what we are aiming for in this book, to borrow Gorringe's phrase, is 'furthering humanity' among the English. We are inviting the English to become more human.

What does inculturation look like?

From what we have discovered so far, we might describe the outcome of inculturation as a 'rooted novelty' which offers 'newness' while at the same time having identifiable continuity and discontinuity with the old realities. Inculturation brings into being a new reality, but one which is rooted *both* in the culture and in the 'gospel'.

Authentic inculturation will then create an exciting 'newness' which is contiguous with the Christian story (whether recognizably 'Christian' from a certain standpoint or not) while using and transforming elements of the foundational culture in a creative manner. The most oft-quoted example, which we have already referred to, is Donovan's work among the Masai (1978).

Having defined what inculturation is, it is worth noting that there are many different ways to reach the goal of integrating faith and culture. Stephen Bevans (2002) offers six models or methods of doing inculturation work – which he calls contextual theology. They all lie somewhere between the poles of faith and culture and in different ways allow greater or lesser importance to each of the two poles. In his book he gives examples for each of the models, including that of Donovan. In the UK some (and probably only some) of the attempts at creating fresh expressions of church are doing interesting inculturation work – for instance on-line or internet churches face questions about how internet culture can be integrated with worship and faith.

On an individual level there is another important outcome of inculturation to be noted. Magesa (2004) calls for that outcome to be 'an integrated spirituality'. He further spells out the meaning of this for Africa, where inculturation means that 'no aspect of life at the physical, psychological, spiritual, institutional or moral level alienates the person. . . . The process should lead to a point where African Christians can . . . live their faith as "truly African and truly Christian," without split personality from divided loyalty.'

This goal is based on a definition of inculturation that goes beyond finding correspondences between faith and culture or adapting faith to culture, as Magesa concludes: 'True inculturation is a deep experience in the life of an individual and the community that occurs when there is a constant search for identification between gospel and culture, and when there is mutual correction and adjustment between them.'

'True inculturation' then regards the future of the faith; the battery produces power; the heart of the 'gospel' beats, giving life.

Both Magesa and Sedmak (2002) make the distinction between official, planned or explicit inculturation and a popular or implicit version of it. So the move from the Book of Common Prayer to the use of *Common Worship* in the Church of England is (partly at least) official inculturation of the liturgy for the modern context, whereas Pentecostal worship exhibits many aspects of popular inculturation. There is a sense in which inculturation is always naturally occurring – existing as 'silent realities' among the people, as Magesa (2004) describes it. Sedmak (2002) notes how implicit inculturation could potentially be 'inconsistent, unjustifiable, or even dangerous', while Magesa adds that this is a possibility even in an explicit inculturation project (2004, p. 189). This is exactly where we find ourselves in this book – realizing that there is an implicit inculturation for any English Christian. Actually we cannot escape some kind of integration of faith and culture, however helpful or unhelpful that is. What I hope to do through this book and the accompanying course is to help readers bring the hidden, implicit inculturation to the surface and examine it afresh in the light of faith, creating a, hopefully, more helpful, explicit inculturation. We will therefore be working in the space between implicit and explicit inculturation, all the while remembering that we are on difficult and contested, if nevertheless holy ground.

Although explicit inculturation, particularly in Roman Catholic thinking, has traditionally been applied to worship and liturgical practice (Gorski, 2004), Magesa (2004) shows how it can be applied as well to behaviour, spirituality and the sacraments. Sedmak (2002) calls for local and regional theologies at a macro level and 'little theologies' at the individual or church community level. These theologies may arise from any social or cultural situation or event, so there is a connection here, as we shall see in Chapter 3, between inculturation work and theological reflection. A wide definition of culture, noted above, does not allow for much that may be outside of the content of inculturation. However, for our purposes in the English context we will be focusing on meaning, values and action or behaviour.

The discussion of intervention requires us now to examine that and other issues at the limits of the inculturation project. We have touched on the question of imperialism and colonization and there are also issues of syncretism which we need to return to.

The limits and critique of inculturation

Is inculturation simply a raiding of the symbols of another culture or religion and employing them in order to further the expansion of the Christian faith (as opposed to humanity)? If so, the charge of imperialism, albeit in a disguised form, is rightly raised. As I have already attempted to make clear, explicit inculturation is not colonizing if we take a translation approach from the incarnation, an approach which affirms 'both universal and particular in a non-alienating way' (Gorringe, 2004). We are therefore required in this study to take absolutely seriously the English context and culture as a possible starting point for the ongoing conversion of the Church.

There is one other issue which the dialectic of universal/ particular and the charge of imperialism raises, and that is the question of revelation. Is revelation only given from God, from above, or is there a revelatory aspect to culture itself? Once again we insist that because of the incarnation (the particular), revelation in Christianity is understood as constantly mediated by culture; thus, unlike in Islam (to be reminded of this chapter's opening quotation from Andrew Walls), there is no culturally fixed element. Revelation is *both* from above *and* from below. Philip Clayton (1999, p. 82) sums up this argument:

> The missiological question offers a continual reminder of this double truth; we believe in God, and hence we are trying to obtain true beliefs about God and God's action, yet every belief we (and others) formulate is always already a cultural project. Because we take culture seriously we are reticent to claim that our particular formulation corresponds to the ultimate fact of divine revelation. Yet because we believe that God has revealed something important about God's nature and purpose in the life and activity of Jesus Christ we cannot give culture (or cultural relativism) the last word.

God does not bypass humanity in revealing himself; if he did we would not have any protection against divine imperatives and consequently the most hard-line of fundamentalisms. Rather the combination of the gospel as revealed in Jesus and the Scriptures mediated by the church (Magesa, 2004) and human culture raised to its heights offers further revelation. Or, to put it another way, 'we can never be certain where Christ is not'. Since this further revelation does not yet exist, we might expect that imagination is required: 'It [inculturation] must, however, be to some degree a "revelation" of a hitherto unknown or un-imagined part of Christ, an unveiling of an astonishing new facet of God's multi-faceted splendour, a gift to the whole church and the whole world, a work of the spirit in our time' (Magesa, 2004, p. 176).

This makes our project a really exciting one, as we don't actually know where it will lead when we set out. It will be about entering and creating new 'worlds' for us to live out of as Christians.

A final question at the margin of inculturation is: where does inculturation stop and syncretism begin? Syncretism is where two religions or cultures come together and the acculturation that goes on between them destroys beyond any recognition the original form of the religions. Examples might be voodoo religions from the Caribbean and to some extent Rastafarianism (Schreiter, 1985, p. 147), where elements are borrowed from Christianity but the resulting religion bears no real relation to it. More recently some so-called 'New Age' cults could fall into this category.

Syncretism could then be defined as an inauthentic inculturation that has destroyed the basic structure and identity of the Christian faith and/or of the receptor culture (Schreiter, 1985). However, there is no clear-cut delineation between what is inculturation and what is syncretism, since the question of *who* defines syncretism remains. The study of the interpretation of language between cultures (a question raised in recent times by the film *Lost in Translation*) has shown the difficulty of communication between speaker and hearer. Schreiter discusses this at length (1997) and concludes that syncretism can only be determined from the side of the hearer, in contrast to the traditional practice of the syncretism being defined by the speaker, sometimes also having the greater 'power'. For instance, it is significant that the African Initiated Kimbanguist Church in former Zaire fought against accusations of syncretism in order eventually to be admitted to the World Council of Churches. In fact, as Hastings points out (1994), the gap between the message of the Bible and its African hearers was much narrower than that for the rationalistic missionaries who brought it. Thus it is the African Initiated Churches such as the Kimbanguists that have the greater claim to authenticity. Around 70 per cent of the English, according to the 2001 census, claim to be Christian. Many 'full-time' Christians dismiss this statistic as meaningless when only around 10 per cent of the population are found worshipping in churches. But perhaps we should take this statement of belonging to the Christian religion much more seriously, because those ticking that census box did have other choices but made a deliberate decision to state their preference for Christianity.

Nevertheless boundaries to inculturation are clearly needed (MPAC, 2004). These could function like the boundaries of a football pitch – drawn to give enough space for proper play, but not drawn so widely that the game is not focused and is therefore unplayable. So we are not about to 'baptize' anything and everything that is English as Christian, but neither can we draw the boundaries so tightly that we cannot recognize any gospel values in many aspects of English culture.

Inculturation, learning and practical theology

The aim of this book is to help readers integrate their faith with English culture. This is inevitably an educative, or learning, process. Such a project is, I would claim, unique – helping people to do explicit inculturation at the grass roots of the church. A further question is then immediately raised – what exactly are the connections, if any, between the work of learning and education and the integration of faith and culture in inculturation?

I believe there are significant connections. The first is via what is known in the field of practical theology as theological reflection. In general the starting point for theological reflection is the same as that of contextual theology – i.e. individual or corporate experience in a particular place and time. Thus Graham, Walton and Ward (2005) define the 'tasks of theological reflection' in three ways:

- asking meaning and identity questions of individual Christians;
- asking meaning and identity questions of the community, which implies an existential question – 'how are we to live faithfully and authentically?' – with the question clearly assuming a context and culture for that faithful living;
- asking how is the faith communicated to a wider culture.

Here then are significant connections between the outcomes of theological reflection and the outcomes of inculturation as we have described them in this chapter, because we are aiming at questions of identity and meaning within a specific cultural context. Graham, Walton and Ward offer seven 'methods' of theological reflection in a similar fashion to Bevans' six 'models' of contextual theology (2002) mentioned above. There are also some connections and overlaps between them; the hermeneutical circle or pastoral cycle (Green, 1990) originated in liberation theology (Bevans' Praxis model) and is utilized in the 'Theology-in-action' method of Graham, Walton and Ward; their seventh method, 'Theology in the Vernacular', follows Schreiter in calling for local, contextual theologies.

It does not require a huge leap of the imagination to turn a theological reflection method into an educational process; in fact several of Graham, Walton and Ward's methods arise from or result in learning programmes. For instance the pastoral cycle is very closely allied to David Kolb's cyclical model of learning with its associated learning styles (1984).

Educational courses, such as the one offered along with this book, can offer the possibility of bridging the gap, identified by both Sedmak and Magesa, between implicit and explicit inculturation. They do this by bringing the hidden assumptions of English culture, held mostly unconsciously by Christians, to the surface for examination and sifting. Yet the question remains as to whether we are introducing a further ideological bias by choosing to use a method of education to address the question of moving from implicit to explicit inculturation.

Gorringe (2004) is convinced that education must not be confined to school or university, but is actually 'co-extensive' with culture. He offers a definition of education from Raymond Williams in which we can discern again the inculturation process: '[education is] the process of giving to the ordinary members of society its full common meanings, and the skills to amend these meanings, in the light of their personal and common experience'.

Following Barth he continues by showing that education is not 'natural' to humanity and will always be an intervention in people's lives in the best sense of that word. Education is about improvement – 'what is *better*' rather than any absolutes, and this 'is a rubric that marks off education from ideology or propaganda'. The learner remains in control while open to the Spirit of God behind the teacher. Education can then be further defined along with its importance to the Church: 'If culture is about value, then education . . . is the place where those values are clarified and debated. The reason that the Church has always been involved in education is precisely because it has an account of the values it believes human beings are called to live by.'

Making educational interventions for the purpose of inculturation, as I am proposing with this book, will therefore be an unfinished process of improvement in the individual and the community. As such, if it remains a process and not an end and takes the non-ideological stance of the incarnation, it will be authentic.

Conclusion

In this chapter we have defined, described and shaped the idea of inculturation around its premise (why?), process (how?), content (what?) and some of its limits. We can therefore offer a working definition of inculturation under the 'pilgrim' and 'indigenizing' principles between the 'poles' of Christian faith and culture. These principles are related to the theological categories of incarnation and conversion (which in turn relate to the historical events of the birth and death of Christ). Christianity is therefore 'translatable' between any culture or cultures in a *process* of inculturation which is ongoing – it is about the future of the faith. The study of English inculturation presented in this book will therefore be a continuing journey rather than expecting an arrival at a distinct end-point.

The outcome of explicit inculturation is a 'rooted novelty' which may be discerned by examining the meaning, values and action or behaviour of the people or peoples involved – in this case the English. It should also lead to an 'integrated spirituality', to use Magesa's term, in the individual. Any ensuing newness from inculturation requires a fluid understanding of revelation and the possible use of the imagination in order for it to be discovered.

2

Englishness

One of the purposes of this book is to get us English, and particularly the Church in England, talking about Englishness; what Englishness means for us as individuals and as a people, including the implications for our place and the landscape we create around us. Any review of the literature on Englishness does not, however, start out on such a project very hopefully.

'Put simply we are terrible at talking about who we are,' claims Paul Kingsnorth in his book *Real England* (2008, p. 14). Kingsnorth argues that for this reason, in combination with the actions of big business and a new moneyed class that wants to protect itself at all costs, England is turning into a homogenized landscape out of touch with itself and destined for a single blandness which drains us of hope. The growth of enormous out-of-town shopping centres, the loss of any uniqueness in our pubs and the way in which our high streets all look the same, conspire together as common enemies in his 'battle against the bland'.

Julian Barnes' vision of his country of birth, as portrayed in his novel *England, England* (1998), is no less troubling and could be seen as a fictionalized version of Kingsnorth's dystopian vision. A thrusting entrepreneur, Sir Jack Pitman, mines the 'Fifty Quintessences of Englishness' (as identified by the best market research) and essentially moves England, its institutions (including the monarchy) and its foundational stories and artefacts into a theme park on the Isle of Wight. The mainland is left to rot, since now the global visitor doesn't have all those troublesome train or road journeys to make between, for instance, London and York. It's all there within easy reach on an even smaller island. And it makes a lot of money.

Outsiders too are often tempted to put pen to paper about the English, perhaps driven on by the fact that we are not so keen on talking about ourselves and there is a lot of humour to be found in such interactions. Perhaps the American Bill Bryson started it all in recent times with his *Notes from a Small Island* (1995), and it's interesting that he has since settled here. Sarah Lyall, another American, married an Englishman and has lived here for over ten years, thus having enough personal observation and reflection to offer *A Field Guide to the English* (2008), which is not quite an anthropological equivalent to the *Book of British Birds*, but is not far off either. Other first- and second-generation immigrants write of their experiences of living in England (and, as we can now call them, their experiences of acculturation and enculturation). So we have Meera Syal, the daughter of immigrants, writing about her childhood growing up in the Black Country in *Anita and Me* (1997), which was also turned into a film. More recently, Shappi Khorsandi, an Iranian, has described in *A Beginner's Guide to Acting English* (2009) her experience of coming to live in London as a small child, first temporarily and then permanently as her father becomes a refugee.

In fact, what Kingsnorth claims might be less true than he thinks – at least at some levels of our society. Certainly if the number of books published about Englishness by English people in the last 10 to 15 years is anything to go by, then actually we are talking about it much, much more. And of course this book is yet another addition to the list.

Jeremy Paxman began this English self-reflection with *The English: A Portrait of a People* (1999). As a broadcaster and public figure Paxman takes a well-researched and wide-ranging look at the English which draws out our national characteristics as well as examining the key institutions and how we ended up where we are today. Paxman therefore neatly encapsulates the three approaches that writers in general take to the subject of Englishness, as pointed out by Ian Bradley, the one theologian to enter the field so far. Although Bradley, a Scotsman, is writing about Britishness, I believe the three approaches he adopts may also be used in the study of Englishness. So we have in his *Believing in Britain: The Spiritual Identity of Britishness* (2007) the assertion that there is first an approach from ethnicity and history – 'where the emphasis is on ancestry, birth and bloodline'. Another option is via citizenship and politics, which 'emphasize legal and political constructs', and finally there is 'the more elusive route of myths, values and customs'.

Of course all these three approaches overlap and interpenetrate each other. These days it is extremely difficult to separate history from myth, as shown by the very title of Edwin Jones' mammoth historical study, *The English Nation: The Great Myth* (2003). History, as we shall see, can create an imagined meaning of England and Englishness which is far removed from the actual historical events. So Michael Wood goes *In Search of England* (2000), taking a series of what he describes in his sub-title as *Journeys into the English Past*, in the first part of his book, through what he himself calls 'Myth and History' and then through particular English texts, people and places. It all adds up to a fascinating study of England and Englishness through the lens of the past.

Billy Bragg, a contemporary singer-songwriter (and, I might add, a personal inspiration to me over the years and in writing this book), takes an avowedly political approach in *The Progressive Patriot: A Search for Belonging* (2006) because he senses that, as a socialist, he needs to recover a proper patriotism about the country of his birth and life from those who would politically take it away from him by force.

Ian Bradley is overall more interested in political approaches but nevertheless deals with national characteristics – indeed he has a chapter each on the English, Celtic (Welsh and Irish), Scottish and multi-cultural (Black and Asian) contributions to what he calls Britishness.

Finally, the Englishwoman Kate Fox, in perhaps the most important background text for my project in this book, undertakes research among the English using the techniques of social anthropology. She points out that anthropology is normally done by going to live with a remote tribe in, say, the Amazonian jungle, but not being predisposed to such a life she stays at home. *Watching the English* (2004) is a fascinating and funny, as well as (as far as I can tell) academically rigorous, study of the English from an anthropological standpoint – it therefore deals almost exclusively with the third approach set out by Bradley of 'myths, values and customs'. We will explore this approach in some detail later in the chapter.

So what is it that has brought about such a flowering of writing and books about England and the English in recent times? I have already hinted at most of the reasons. Globalization has had just as much impact on our own place and people as anywhere else in the world (and perhaps, in this current period 'after Empire', even more so). We cannot lead isolationist lives when we use Chinese goods and Japanese electricals, eat green beans from Kenya and are affected by the collapse of the sub-prime mortgage market in the United States. With globalization has come continued immigration into this country and in encountering the 'other' – that is, anyone who looks or acts differently from ourselves – we are bound to ask questions about ourselves. All of which leads us to the most sensitive question raised by the writing of this book.

Paxman, Kingsnorth and Bragg are not the only ones interested in recovering a sense of Englishness. There are others who do so from different motives, and there is clearly a spectrum or continuum which we need to be aware of when discussing Englishness. A quarterly magazine called *This England*, which is around 40 years old now, celebrates all things 'English', but one suspects that Englishness is defined by the magazine's editors in a particular way. For instance, they have a series on the meaning of English surnames, but the names chosen are exclusively of Anglo-Saxon or Norman origin. In the same genre, the charity the Steadfast Trust (<www.steadfasttrust.org.uk>) advocates for the education, legal rights and understanding of the cultural heritage of the 'ethnic English', whatever that term means – and if it does mean just the 'white' English, then that connects it with other right-wing organizations.

More sinister is the English Defence League, formed in 2009 to 'combat radical Islam' in England. They claim that anyone is welcome in their ranks and they are not racist, but others – including several public figures – have called this claim into question. They certainly act in very provocative and unhelpful ways by marching regularly in our most multi-racial cities; as Billy Bragg has said (on a concert tour in 2010), they truly don't know what it means to be English. Also there are those on the extremes of the far right who claim the flag of St George and St George's Day as their own, and who are overtly racist. Such people are particularly well portrayed in Shane Meadows' semi-autobiographical film *This is England* (2006). Set in the early 1980s, the film portrays an initially peace-loving and non-racist skinhead gang divided by a new strongly racist leader, 'Combo', just released from prison. He splits the members and eventually badly beats up the one black member of the original gang, prompting the 12-year-old hero of the film, Shaun, to throw the Union Jack into the sea in the poignant last scene. Needless to say, the spirit of Combo lives on today in many far-right organizations, including of course the British National Party.

And yet the Archbishop of York, John Sentamu, who is of Ugandan origin, has called for a renewed celebration of all things English and even asks whether St George's Day might become a public holiday (2009). There is a way to recover England and Englishness from the racists and the more of us who can do that the better.

All of this confirms my conviction that we are on holy ground when discussing Englishness. It is a place not to enter lightly or without much thought – we need to 'take off our shoes' here and tread carefully. Matters of faith and culture, the Roman Catholic missiologist Anthony Gittins states (2000), are 'matters of life and death', as I hinted at in Chapter 2. Any discussion of Englishness can lead us to embrace life more fully, to further humanity, or can take us into death and darkness. In this chapter then, we will indeed tread carefully as we review our history (albeit a largely mythic history), touch on political questions and discover the cultural heart of Englishness.

Englishness, history and myth

Where do we start with the question of history? Characteristically, and a little bizarrely, the British National Party (BNP) go back to the last Ice Age in the search for 'indigenous' origins. Since this is prehistory, however, it would be difficult to impute any notions of nationhood to the people who lived on our island at that time. The BNP recognize of course that successive 'migrations of the Celts, Anglo-Saxons, Danes, Norse and closely related kindred peoples' also make up our identity,[1] but the hidden agenda here is clearly both race and colour, since they have conveniently forgotten the first period of written history about Britain – when the Romans expanded their empire here and lived on our soil for centuries. No doubt many did leave with the collapse of that Empire, but their presence, impact and legacy has also stayed with us.

It is not unreasonable, therefore, to claim that historically England is a multi-ethnic mix of peoples and that this is part of its unique identity. Certainly this is the view of both Billy Bragg and Robert Beckford, a black theologian from Birmingham, as well as of David Miles, author of possibly the definitive recent archaeological work on the ethnic origins of people in these islands, *The Tribes of Britain* (2006). All these authors refer to the period after the Romans left Britain (traditionally known as the Dark Ages as there seems to have been very little literary activity in the period) when a series of invasions from continental Europe into the east of our island pushed the Celtic Britons to the fringes of the west. This is the 'origin myth of the English people' (Bragg, 2006, p. 49) for which we are indebted to the Venerable Bede, a monk working in Jarrow in the seventh and eighth centuries CE. His *Ecclesiastical History of the English People* (731), admittedly politically biased (in those days ecclesiastical and national histories were much more intertwined), nevertheless

---

[1] Mission Statement by Nick Griffin, 30 September 2008; quoted at <http://scotland.bnp.org.uk/category/the-quiet-revolution/>, accessed 26 November 2009.

provides us with the first account of how England developed a national identity.

Members of three races – Angles, Saxons and Jutes – came from what we know as Germany and settled from Kent to Northumbria. As Bragg points out, it was very difficult for Bede to tell the story of this settlement of England from the point of view of any one of these tribes – he wanted a unifying story and gave each of them equal significance: 'Thanks to Bede, the very earliest concepts of what it means to be English are founded on immigration, multi-ethnic diversity and inclusion' (2006, p. 52).

Beckford claims it was Bede's Christianity which enabled him to provide a unifying narrative for English identity which still resonates today for the son of an immigrant such as himself:

> The story of the forging of England as an entity, with the assistance of Christianity, has much in it to inspire us today. The importance of religion establishing a shared experience on which a nation could be built is a case in point. But this history is also important today because of the ongoing battle over what it means to be English. During my lifetime, I have witnessed Enoch Powell, Margaret Thatcher and even Gordon Brown try to fix English identity as if it had natural boundaries. The Dark Ages and the thread of Christianity running through it point to a possible alternative, the sense of England as a fluid idea, a place where diverse peoples live together, syncretize ideas and create new cultures. This Dark Age idea is an image of national identity that I, the son of immigrants, can readily embrace.[2]

Two artefacts from this very same period underline the multi-ethnic point being made here. The beautiful Lindisfarne Gospels were created by monks on Holy Island who, according to Beckford, 'appropriated cultural symbols from across the known world and wove them into the artwork'. Bragg mentions the Franks Casket, a small whalebone box dating from between 650

---

[2] Robert Beckford writing on the *Guardian* website, 23 January 2009: <http://www.guardian.co.uk/commentisfree/belief/2009/jan/23/christianity-religion-national-identity>, accessed 26 November 2009.

and 750 CE, whose four carved sides show images from 'Christian, Roman, Jewish and Germanic culture, each surrounded by a Scandinavian runic inscription' (2006, p. 53).

During the seventh to the ninth centuries, Angles, Saxons and Jutes were in the process of becoming unified, and we know them now in the result of that unification as the Anglo-Saxons – or 'the people of the hyphen' as Bragg puts it. He remarks on the significance of the hyphen in so early an ethnic identifier in comparison to the usually singular origin myths from other places and peoples around the world – 'the hyphen in Anglo-Saxon is symbolic of our ancient multi-cultural traditions' (2006, p. 55).

King Offa fairly successfully ruled the Anglo-Saxons in England south of the Humber (from 757 to 796 CE), but his later successor Alfred (ruling from 871 to 899 CE) called himself King of all the Anglo-Saxons. Alfred, though, had to deal with another people who saw an opportunity for a better life by coming to England; these were the Danes, or as they are perhaps better known – and feared – the Vikings. Thus the kingdom had to accommodate once again, this time to the increasing Danish influence, right up until the Norman invasion in 1066.

There is no doubt that the events of 1066 are definitive in many ways for Englishness, but for me it's not so much the historical events in themselves but the myths that they create that are important for our study of the origins of Englishness. Two important myths emerge from the time of the Norman Conquest of England.

The first, interestingly and suggestively, is the legend of King Arthur, supposedly king of the 'Britons' (those people inhabiting the island at the end of the Roman period and into the sixth century), which is championed by, among others, Geoffrey of Monmouth in the century following the Conquest (Wood, 2000). It is not surprising that at a time when the national identity is being reformed after a major invasion, those in power develop and co-opt the already existent oral tradition about Arthur for the purpose of strengthening their hold on the nation; Michael Wood even suggests Geoffrey's purpose was to 'prove him [Arthur] dead and reinvent him as a tourist event' (2000, p. 25).

There is very little historical evidence for the existence of Arthur and this is not the place to replay those arguments (although we are going to look in more detail at another foundational English myth in a later chapter where the question of historicity will have to be dealt with again). Nevertheless there are two things worth noting about the importance of Arthur for understanding ourselves. The stories of Arthur are based in the south (and west) of the land and establish the 'living bond between the Britons and the English' (Wood, 2000, p. 42, quoting Faulkner Jones' *The English Spirit*), thus mediating to us a sense of place, identity and continuity with that period of our history when the Roman Empire was breaking up and the Anglo-Saxons were arriving and threatening to take over. Arthur defends the western Celts against those who would become 'the English' and so the myth helps to negotiate and confirm that boundary for us.

More importantly, perhaps, the myth arises at a time when the Normans have invaded and the country is under a new subjugation. There is a distinct possibility, therefore, that the Arthur legends function to help the people make sense of and assimilate the situation they find themselves in under their Norman rulers, a motif we can also trace in how the arrival of the Normans came to be understood historically in the later medieval period and beyond.

The 'myth of the Norman Yoke' is probably the most familiar myth to many of us – some would say it is the central myth of our history. It emerged most strongly in the period after the Reformation and during the Civil War (and it informs later versions of the Robin Hood myth, as we shall see). Michael Wood defines it simply (2000, p. 10):

> England had free institutions before 1066, which were lost to William the Conqueror. All laws made since the conquest were therefore illegal: so from 1066 till 1642 (and indeed afterwards) the English lived under the Norman Yoke. English law had been superseded by laws written in Norman French and interpreted by Norman

lawyers; the Old English custom of local government, with hearings in the vernacular, had been done away with; the feudal system had dispossessed the free-born English.

Wood traces how the myth was exposed by historians in the twentieth century who understood that it had 'been created in the sixteenth century to justify and underline the break with Rome' (2000, p. 13). Yet he is also prepared to reassess it now as it seems there is real historical evidence to support it. The Norman minority (there were 20–30,000 of them compared with 1.5 million Anglo-Saxons) did effect a complete takeover of the land and its institutions from its Anglo-Saxon masters without interacting with the original population very much for many generations. Thus the harsh realities of the Norman occupation fuelled subversive elements and radicalism over the ensuing centuries, right up to the time of the Civil War – and particularly when economic times were hard. Wood again (2000, p. 17):

> There seems to be a case for thinking that the Norman Yoke is a continuous literary and folk theme from the eleventh century to the Tudors, continuing on to the radicals in the seventeenth century who picked it up and ran with it. A theme which survived till our own times, one of the most potent English myths.

And yet we are an English nation using the English language and not a French one using their tongue. English was clearly the lower-class language in the early Norman period, but Wood notes how English vernacular literature revived in the fourteenth century – a 'demonstration of the ability of English to stay underground and metamorphose. Today we are still an English nation and not French' (2000, p. 18).

I came across a real example of this recently when I was Priest-in-Charge of St Leodegarius' Church in Basford, Nottingham. It is one of only four churches in England dedicated to this saint who, when you read his history, is clearly from northern France – Norman country. It seems fairly clear that our church was built by the Normans on a strategically important river crossing point outside the northern entrance to Nottingham. But what was fascinating was the inability of most people – even some in the church – to pronounce the name Leodegarius with any kind of accuracy. I also came across many interesting attempts to spell it. Every kind of diminutive was used, while inside church we referred mostly to St Leo's – even though there is another St Leo (usually also designated the Great) with whom our saint could be confused. I also discovered that St Leger (as in the fairly well known horse race of that name) is essentially the English way of pronouncing Leodegarius. Thus the tensions introduced by the Norman invasion still play out in the way that, as the established Church, we stick with the full Norman dedication, but then subvert it at all sorts of different levels through our language.

So the last full invasion and subjugation of our land over a thousand years ago is still significant for our identity today. But was it a case of the aristocratic and organized Normans taking over weak Anglo-Saxon institutions and laying the foundations for our later greatness? Or was it a version of ethnic cleansing which oppressed a people with perfectly serviceable laws and an equitable society that needed to be rediscovered by later generations? Both views can be held, and as in most debates of this kind there's probably an element of truth on both sides – but, as Wood concludes, 'we never forget' (2000, p. 22) and we wonder what might have been.

I think we can conclude, however, by reiterating the words of Robert Beckford: this very brief review of the mythical history of our origins shows us that England is a 'fluid idea, a place where diverse peoples live together, syncretise ideas and create new cultures'.

But what of Christianity in the history, mythical or otherwise, of our nation? Anyone who has sung William Blake's hymn 'Jerusalem' taps into something very deep in the English which we need to explore – that somehow we are a chosen nation visited and blessed by God in Christ. For many, that is enough to make us Christian, whether we go near a church or not.

Let's remind ourselves of the words of the hymn:

> And did those feet in ancient time
> Walk upon England's mountains green?
> And was the holy Lamb of God
> On England's pleasant pastures seen?
> And did the countenance divine
> Shine forth upon our clouded hills?
> And was Jerusalem builded here
> Among those dark satanic mills?
>
> Bring me my bow of burning gold!
> Bring me my arrows of desire!
> Bring me my spear! O clouds, unfold!
> Bring me my chariot of fire!
> I will not cease from mental fight,
> Nor shall my sword sleep in my hand,
> Till we have built Jerusalem
> In England's green and pleasant land.

The first verse refers to the legend that arose around the town of Glastonbury, that Christ himself visited there as a child. The story has to be laid alongside a whole mythology which developed around Glastonbury between the tenth and twelfth centuries, as is outlined by Michael Wood (2000, p. 44). Wood claims that the English don't have foundational, or what he calls 'real' myths, when compared with the ancient sagas of Norse, Celtic or Hindu mythologies, because our history is relatively recent. After the conversion of the country to Christianity it was inevitable that a new mythology would arise, and this was focused on Glastonbury – as the chief holy place of the nation, at least until the Reformation.

The idea that England and its Church was blessed by Christ from the very beginning through the place of Glastonbury is first hinted at in the tenth-century *Life of Saint Dunstan*, where our ancient church is described as being built 'by no human skill' (Wood, 2000, p. 57). From that point on Glastonbury, focused on its abbey, grew to be at the holy heart of England alongside the development of the Anglo-Saxon nation state. In this sense, allied as they are with the West Saxon kings of England, the legends of our Christian origins associated with Glastonbury are truly *English* (2000, p. 61).

Many of the more familiar legends associated with Glaston-bury, such as King Arthur, the Holy Grail and the visit of Joseph of Arimathea, however, come from the twelfth century onwards. They developed with the flowering of the Arthurian legends, as we saw above, but were particularly boosted by the 'discovery' in 1191 of Arthur's grave there. Of course the Abbey was destroyed during the Reformation, but the legends flowered again in the Victorian period, particularly among the pre-Raphaelites, maintaining their vitality through the twentieth century until today, when there are a wide variety spiritualities on display in the town.

The important point for this study is that Glastonbury points to our Christian origins; as Wood states, 'it was holy *before the Catholic Church* . . . It was the primordial British shrine, free of sectarian taint' (2000, p. 67, his italics). So Glastonbury exists as a metaphor – or perhaps better, is part of the English imagination which is built up through our understanding of our mythic history. There is a sense of the blessedness of our land by God through Christ from *the beginning.*

Still, the Christian reader may have in mind a question at this point: what has all this talk of our mythical origins as a Christian people got to do with the gospel and salvation today? It would be easy to write it all off as sub-Christian myth. But, having worked in Africa, my inclination is not to do so. Kwame Bediako (2008), in one of his last articles before his untimely death, argues strongly that the gospel connections between African 'primal' religions and culture and the Christian faith, focused as it is on the person of Christ, should be taken abso-lutely seriously. We should not therefore denigrate our own 'primal religion', since that religion has been Christian almost from the very beginning of the Christian faith itself.

We could continue to review Englishness through histor-ical developments beyond the medieval period and consider the way that history soon turns into myth in popular culture (think of Shakespeare, Rowan Atkinson's *Blackadder* comedy series and war films), but space docs not allow us. One of the reasons history turns to myth and legend is of course the politics of nationhood, and it is to that we now turn.

Englishness and the politics of Britishness

In this chapter we have already faced up to a political question raised by the very fact of wanting to explore and then celebrate English identity. Politics is not a primary interest of this book, but it would be remiss not to cover the question in any further detail at all.

However, my issue with spending too much time with the question of politics is two-fold. First, if we explore the political and civic institutions on the surface of our public life we quickly come to recognize the mythical history and the national values behind them. Billy Bragg (2006) trumpets the continuity between the development between 1215 and 1225 of the Magna Carta, the history of English radicalism (e.g. Luddites and Chartists, etc.), and the birth of the National Health Service in 1948. He understands the development of the principles enshrined in the Magna Carta of 'government by consent and equality under the law' as arising from the English character and shaping it ever since. As we shall see, fairness and fair play are key values among the English, values which also drive us to stand up to unchecked power and support the underdog. So our political institutions are *illustrative* of cultural values and norms.

We can develop this same point by looking at a speech made by David Blunkett MP in 2005, when he helpfully explored the politics of identity and notions of Englishness within Britishness.[3] He notes, as we have, the historical multi-national and multi-ethnic nature of English people and observes that interpretation and understanding of our history is no closed book. Examples

---

[3] 'A New England: English Identity within Britain', speech to the Institute for Public Policy Research, 14 March 2005, available at <www.efdss.org/newengland.pdf>, accessed 7 September 2009.

of what he 'would celebrate on St. George's day' are English rural and urban landscapes and the sea, the English musical, poetical and democratic traditions, English radicalism and English humour. A mixture, as we might expect, of 'high' culture, politics and values. Thus he calls for the best kind of local, civic engagement and concludes by affirming that:

> We can build a new sense of English identity, finding its place among the plural identities of the United Kingdom and supporting a wider sense of Britishness. Englishness can be experienced, asserted and celebrated in the fabric of our existence as a community: in our habits, casts of mind, the culture that we daily create and re-create. We can find it in our traditions of fairness and civic duty and in our spirit of imagination and invention. In this way we can overcome bigotry, insularity and hostility.

Blunkett's placing of Englishness within Britishness leads to a further point. It is Britain and Britishness that are the more important political constructs which can hold together the 'hyphenated' nature of the people of these islands. There is good survey evidence, quoted by Bradley (2008, p. 20), that people in ethnic minority communities identify more closely with Britishness than Englishness, but this seems to me no less a reason to celebrate our cultural diversity. Where I depart from Bradley is in his overall task to turn the helpful political construct of Britishness into a spiritual, religious and cultural project, as I am not convinced it can bear the weight of what he is expecting of it. As Wood notes (2000, p. 91), 'we became Britons in the eighteenth century' with the building of empire and a new history – from the beginning Britishness was politically useful and it remains so at that level.

Thus, when Bradley turns to the importance of values as defining Britain's identity (2008, p. 62) he states that the most often cited values are 'creativity, adaptability, openness, tolerance, liberty, fairness, decency, fair play, courtesy, civic duty, forbearance and magnanimity'. These, as we shall see, are very close to the defining characteristics of the English and therefore I am not sure quite how they are attributed to the whole of Britain. Where Bradley is more helpful is in suggesting some political interventions that could make a difference in Britain, such as redesigning the Union flag and emphasizing pan-British institutions such as the monarchy and the BBC, as well as developing localized citizenship programmes.

Defining the cultural heart of Englishness: an anthropology of the English

We are now in a position to turn to the key text in the background of this book: Kate Fox's *Watching the English: The Hidden Rules of English Behaviour* (2004). Politics on the surface of public life, and history and myth behind that, can take us so far in understanding Englishness, but my contention is that there is an unconscious Englishness or culture which drives our everyday behaviour (and therefore of course our public life). Without knowledge of these hidden drivers we cannot understand the uniqueness of the English, and, by extension for English readers, ourselves. For help here we turn to the discipline of anthropology.

In Chapter 1 we looked at the wide range of definitions of culture and how to describe it. Robert Schreiter's semiotic approach to culture led to the discipline of anthropology and so, inevitably, to Kate Fox's anthropological research among the English. Whereas sociology deals with the organization of human society, anthropology digs deeper to scientifically study the origins of human behaviour and culture.

Fox begins her book with some interesting claims for her three-year research project, which sets out to 'discover the hidden, unspoken rules of English behaviour, and what those rules tell us about our national identity' (2004, p. 2). She is convinced there is such a thing as Englishness and that it has not been entirely lost in the throes of modernity, globalization or even post-modernity. Therefore there ought to be, in Englishness, what she calls *commonalities* that 'cut across class, age, sex, region, sub-cultures and other social boundaries'. She points out that 'ethnographic dazzle' often prevents the researcher from getting beneath surface superficialities in behaviour.

For instance, she discovers that English leather-clad bikers and (presumably) woolly-cardiganed members of the Women's Institute actually behave similarly or abide by the same rules when you get beneath the surface of how they physically present themselves.

Culture can be likened to language (in fact the two are closely related). So, just as it is difficult for native speakers to explain the grammatical rules of their own language, neither can they explain the 'rituals, customs and traditions of their culture'. In fact, in my experience of crossing cultures it is not a very sensible thing to ask directly why a certain thing is done in the way it is. Such a question can elicit a hostile response, as it is subtly perceived as an attack on the listener's core identity; more likely, it will receive something like the response which is often trotted out to curious Wazungu (white foreigners) in Tanzania in the wonderfully poetic phrase, '*hivyo ilivyo ndivyo*', or to translate, 'that's just the way it is [mate!]'.

It is the task of anthropologists, as Fox understands it, to explore the unconscious reasons why we do what we do – even down to the most obvious things, like going to work in work clothes rather than the ones we sleep in (since it would never occur to the San bushmen in Namibia that such a distinction existed). But it's not easy being an anthropologist because it entails becoming a *participant observer* within the culture being studied. Participant observation requires the researcher to embed herself in the culture she is studying for long enough that she can become part of it while at the same time remaining detached enough to make scientific observations about it. It is perhaps the ultimate conjunction of the subjective and objective modes of human enquiry and as such quite difficult to do well. Too much subjectivity and the temptation is to be subsumed by the host culture, too much objectivity and nothing much of any interest may be discovered. Nevertheless, as Fox comments: 'while participant observation has its limitations, this rather uneasy combination of involvement and detachment is still the best method we have for exploring the complexities of human cultures, so it will have to do' (2004, p. 4).

Fox then defines what she means by the 'rules' she is setting out to discover. These turn out to be 'the normal or usual state of things', thus allowing for exceptions and difference among patterns of behaviour that are generally common (2004, p. 9); she points out that actually the best rules have exceptions that 'prove the rule'. The elucidation of English behaviour rules in her research will lead, she hopes, to an understanding and definition of English culture – with culture being 'the sum of a social group's patterns of behaviour, customs, way of life, ideas, beliefs and values' (2004, p. 10). This is pretty close to the definition we gleaned from Gorringe and others in Chapter 1.

Fox then addresses the important question of what is universal across all human cultures and what, beyond these universals, might be peculiar and unique about Englishness. For instance, there is in all cultures 'a system of social status and methods of indicating it', but the English class system has some characteristics not found anywhere else (2004, p. 12). She goes on to note that class in England is so pervasive an issue that it needs to be discussed in all her chapters rather than have one of its own.

It is important too that Fox addresses the question of race at the start of her work, as we have had to in different ways. She is clear that '*by definition* ethnic minorities are included in any attempt to define Englishness' (2004, p. 16, her italics). This is because:

- Ethnic minorities have definitely contributed to the 'grammar' of Englishness, despite, as we have noted, preferring to refer to themselves as British not English.
- Some (and only some) have so acculturated to their adoptive home that they have become more 'English' than the English. (There is a similar phenomenon in the particularly 'proper' grammatical use of the English language in India.) This gets us beyond race, as defined by skin or hair colour or country of origin. There are undoubtedly, therefore, 'degrees' of Englishness.
- Consequently immigrants have more choice than their native English counterparts as to which parts of English culture they choose to take on (despite, according to Fox at least, the

apparent hegemony of the host culture when acculturation happens). That is, they can be more conscious about the choices they make as to which English behaviours they accommodate to (as in Khorsandi, 2009) – unlike the 'native' population, for whom the reasons we do certain things remain hidden.

• There is therefore nothing value-laden about Englishness. It is not right or wrong to adopt it or not – no one has to learn it in order to be a better person!

And here Fox reaches one of the limits of her work, a limit which is important for us. She is attempting description not prescription. For our purposes her description is extremely useful because it encompasses all of English society in the early twenty-first century. Our task later in the book will be to lay this description alongside the 'gospel' or the Christian faith and reflect on what might emerge as prescriptive for our self-understanding, attitudes and behaviour as the Christian English.

Finally Fox touches on the Britishness question (2004, p. 21) and concludes, as we have, that Britain is a political construct; that the cultures making up Britain are not identical and so cannot really be joined together under Britishness; and that, finally, the use of Britishness as a term is often really a cover for wanting to use Englishness instead (but perhaps not having the courage to do so).

She is therefore ready to embark on the project of metaphorically 'sequencing the English cultural genome' (2004, p. 22).

While I have given in this section a very full summary of Fox's introductory chapter, because it deals with all the preliminary issues and even objections to her project, it is not my intention to go into much more detail about the content of most of the chapters of her book. Suffice to say it is as comprehensive a survey of English life and custom as I could imagine, covering as it does conversation codes (semiotics again) to do with weather, grooming, humour, class, mobile phones and pubs, along with behaviour codes in relation to home, transport, work, play, dress, food, sex and rites of passage. It is a fascinating and often hilarious read and I fully recommend it.

For our purposes now though we can jump to her conclusions as she brings all the disparate fieldwork data together to define Englishness in her final chapter. What she comes up with are ten characteristics of Englishness. One of these is a central core that pervades everything else, while there are three groups of three other characteristics. In the rest of this chapter I shall outline and illustrate these ten characteristics and their place in the map of the English cultural genome. As I do this, I hope you the reader, if English, can check whether you identify with these findings and if not, whether you have noticed them in the English people that you know or are familiar with. Let me make it clear that it is the *combination* of these characteristics that defines Englishness. No doubt we could find some of them present in other countries and nationalities, but we are claiming there is something unique about the English through this mixture of reflexes, outlooks and values.

Inevitably here I shall have to quote large chunks of Fox's final chapter (2004, pp. 400–16), but I hope to add some of my own illustrations and thoughts, as well as the occasional corroboration from Jeremy Paxman and Billy Bragg.

The core: social dis-ease

The English are chronically socially inhibited. Even writing these words and contemplating setting out a full description of this dis-ease seems to be difficult and inhibiting for an Englishman like myself. It is painful to be shown your own culture, but let's remember we are being descriptive here. We seem to be 'socially challenged' in social interaction, we are embarrassed, insular, awkward, perverse, oblique and fearful of intimacy. For some reason Ricky Gervais' sitcom *The Office* comes to mind, which I have to say I found so excruciating that at times it was too difficult to watch.

The English have two reactions to this core issue – the one I have just experienced, which is to become 'over-polite, buttoned up and awkwardly restrained', or on the other hand to become 'loud, loutish, crude, violent and generally obnoxious'. Our famous 'English reserve' and our infamous 'English hooliganism', states Fox, are two sides of the same coin.

Connected within this core is our love of privacy. Every year or two there is a court case where neighbours have come to violence, and even in extreme cases murder, over boundary disputes between their properties. The Englishman's home, as we shall explore in more detail later, is very much his castle.

When travelling by air, I really like the moments just after take-off and just before landing. If you have a window seat (and you are flying in daylight), you can see the layout of the houses and their gardens from a height that enables you still to be nosy. I once flew from Dar es Salaam in Tanzania to Johannesburg in South Africa. Flying out over Dar all I could see were miles of corrugated iron roofs, but coming into Jo'burg (from a certain direction, no doubt) there were blue dots everywhere – swimming pools! What always strikes me coming in to land in London (from anywhere in Europe or the rest of the world) is how separate and individual the houses are. Yes, there are occasional blocks of flats, but the rule is miles and miles of houses, with fences and gardens front and back.

Fox states that we treat our national dis-ease with any number of 'props and facilitators', such as pubs, clubs, weather-speak and pets. Most clergy will know that if you really want to get to know your English parishioners on arrival in a new parish, then buy a dog and take it for walks at the same time as everyone else. Conversations will take place through the pet. Puppies (and perhaps babies) are even better.

Three groups of characteristics circle the core of what Fox describes as the English cultural genome (she has a diagram of this on p. 410, which she is characteristically self-deprecating about). The groups are 'reflexes', 'outlooks' and 'values', and they are all interrelated in the diagram. The reflexes are humour, moderation and hypocrisy; the outlooks are empiricism, Eeyorishness and class-consciousness; and the values are fair play, courtesy and modesty. I will describe each of these in turn now.

Humour

Reflexes are 'deeply ingrained impulses, knee-jerk responses, default modes', things we do without thinking – 'the cultural equivalents of laws of gravity'. So humour is ubiquitous in English life – it is a constant feature of our interactions, in contrast to other cultures where it is confined to certain times and places. 'Virtually all English conversations and social inter- actions involve at least some degree of banter, teasing, irony, wit, mockery, wordplay, satire, understatement, humorous self-deprecation, sarcasm, pomposity pricking or just silliness' (Fox, 2004, p. 402).

One of my fondest memories was going as a teenager with my grandfather to watch England play Test cricket at the Headingley ground in Leeds. I remember sitting on a hard wooden bench on the west side of the ground, where with any luck we would be in front of a bunch of lads from Barnsley or some such place who were in a cricket team of their own. They knew each other and the game well and had come to have fun – fuelled, needless to say, by copious amounts of beer. At about three o'clock in the afternoon their corporate banter reached its zenith and it was naturally and almost beautifully hilarious, although by six o'clock it had inevitably dissolved into silliness.

There is a long English tradition of satirical humour which subverts and exposes authority (the magazines *Punch* and *Private Eye* for example) and which is very peculiar to us. Amazingly some English humour does travel – although I suspect wordless humour such as that of Rowan Atkinson's Mr Bean travels better. You still have to be very careful though, as Fox points out; much English humour is used to cover up awkward situations: 'when in doubt, joke.' My wife and I were once travelling in a foreign country with a rather absent-minded colleague, a native of that country, and I suppose we thought, since we had been together for some time, that the relationship had developed to such a level that we could try some humour when our friend's forgetfulness occurred again. But 'You'd forget your head, Peter, if it wasn't screwed on' was not the best response we could have made! It took a couple of weeks to get over that one.

Fox describes our national catchphrase as the one word: 'Typical!' We shall be working with this phrase later in the book and once you have heard yourself say it, it is remarkable how often you find it comes out. It rains all the Bank Holiday weekend – typical! The toast lands butter-side down – typical! The government puts up taxes, again – typical!

Moderation

The English are a people of the middle way and it is no surprise that our national church's DNA – its founding mantra if you like, going back to Richard Hooker – is that of the *via media*. We tried some extremism in the English Civil War and the Commonwealth that followed it, but when Christmas was essentially banned by the Puritan-influenced government, it all got too much for us and the status quo was soon restored.

Most elections in our country are fought over who will win, in that marvellously elusive phrase, 'middle England'. Needless to say, straying too far from the centre in politics is usually a disaster, a point Paxman makes several times (e.g. 1999, p. 5).

It seems that even advertisers and marketing executives have done their English anthropology these days. I saw recently an advert for a type of margarine that sold itself exactly as a middle way, a compromise between being essentially unhealthy for you and tasting like butter and yet powerfully healthy with a low fat content.

I wonder if you have ever thought about what is going on in the annual Oxford v. Cambridge boat race. According to the boat race website, 'On 12 March 1829, Cambridge sent a challenge to Oxford and thus the tradition was born which has continued to the present day, where the loser of the previous year's race challenges the opposition to a re-match.'[4]

---

[4] <http://theboatrace.org/article/introduction>, accessed 10 December 2009.

Apparently, as I write, Cambridge currently lead the 'series' by 79 to Oxford's 75. So in over 150 'races' one team has just four more wins than the other. Is this a fix? Absolutely not, *and* I can guarantee that neither side will ever be more than about ten races ahead of the other. This is England. 'Don't rock the boat' is the saying we love to use to espouse moderation – literally in this case.

Hypocrisy

And so to hypocrisy! I think the best example of this is the summer game we invented and which I have already alluded to – cricket. On the surface it looks genteel and quintessentially polite. The players wear white, the colour of purity, batsmen are clapped in and out – and if they are out early, shouts of 'bad luck, old man' can be heard. But scratch the surface of the game and a bowler is trying at the very least to intimidate and at worst to seriously injure the batsman with an extremely hard round object. Fielders, and especially the wicket-keeper, keep up a constant barrage of loud comments to team-mates about their own fantastic performances, and under-the-breath comments to the batsmen about their all too obvious shortcomings and no doubt their dubious parentage. Just like English life then.

Fox doesn't think, though, that our hypocrisy is deliberate, 'a calculated attempt to deceive others'. Rather, as one of her reflexes, it seems to be a matter of 'unconscious, collective *self*-deception' (2004, p. 404, her italics). The best example for her is the way we deceive ourselves over class – on the surface preferring 'polite egalitarianism', which is a cover for or denial of the class-consciousness present in every interaction between English people. For Paxman, English hypocrisy has its serious side: he notes the English people's 'extraordinary capacity for believing they can have it both ways' (1999, p. 101). He points out that while the abortion debate continues to rage in America, leading often to violence, we prefer quietly to ignore the fact that one in four pregnancies in our country ends in termination. I suppose Mike Leigh's film *Vera Drake* (2004) deals with the agony that is created in the midst of this peculiar kind of English hypocrisy – whatever you think about abortion.

Empiricism

This is the first of Fox's outlooks. By outlooks she means the way we uniquely look at the world and understand and structure it in our minds – what some academics call our 'world-view'.

By empiricism Fox is not describing the formal philosophical idea that all knowledge is derived from what we can experience with our five senses alone, but is using the term in the broader, more informal sense that the English look at the world with a 'stubborn preference for the factual, concrete and common sense'. Perhaps the word pragmatism sums it up, and of course it often joins up with our preferred kind of humour – as exemplified in the catchphrase 'Oh, come off it!'

Paxman quotes George Steiner on the English: 'If the Lord God came to England and started expounding his beliefs, you know what they'd say? They'd say "Oh, come off it!"' (1999, p. 189). And in another place he quotes a character in an Alan Bennett play, *The Old Country*: 'We're [the English] conceived in irony. We float in it from the womb. It's the amniotic fluid. It's the silver sea. It's the waters at their priest-like task, washing away guilt and purpose and responsibility. Joking, but not joking. Caring but not caring. Serious, but not serious' (1999, p. 18).

I know I said earlier on I would not refer much to Fox's intervening chapters, but as an English chip lover myself I will just refer to what she says about chips in relation to empiricism – and perhaps prove my own pragmatism in the process. Despite chips being invented in Belgium, apparently 90 per cent of the English eat chips at least once per week. She quotes a particular respondent to some focus-group research: 'The chip is down to earth. It's basic, it's simple in a good way, which is why we like the chip. We have that quality and it's a good quality . . . This is what we are – no faffing about' (2004, p. 321).

Need I say more?

Eeyorishness

This is a term which is used extensively by Fox, and interestingly also by Jeremy Paxman (1999, p. 14, though he spells it with an 'e' in the middle). Eeyore is of course the gloomy, pessimistic donkey in A. A. Milne's *Winnie the Pooh* stories. Here is Eeyore in conversation with Christopher Robin, a conversation, perhaps inevitably, about the weather:

> 'It's snowing still,' said Eeyore gloomily.
> 'So it is.'
> 'And freezing.'
> 'Is it?'
> 'Yes,' said Eeyore. 'However,' he said, brightening up a little, 'we haven't had an earthquake lately.'

While moaning is clearly a national characteristic, Fox is clear that there is something distinctive about the way we do it: 'we never complain to or confront the source of our discontent, but only whinge endlessly to each other . . . But it is socially therapeutic – highly effective as a facilitator of social interaction and bonding' (2004, p. 405).

Perhaps there is a lesson here for me, as one of my professional roles and interests is in the training and development of clergy. One of the moans that we have as trainers about clergy is their propensity to moan when they get together. Yet if we understood the need to have a good moan as just a way of breaking the ice in a meeting (and breaking the ice is an interesting metaphor in itself!), perhaps we could get down to business more quickly and easily. And of course, as Fox points out, it is highly enjoyable, as almost all social moaning is 'humorous *mock*-moaning' (2004, p. 405, her emphasis) and it offers an opportunity for displays of wit and banter.

Once again, then, Eeyorishness as an outlook ties up with the humour reflex. And its characteristic phrase is the same: 'Typical!'

Class-consciousness

One of the things we have heard consistently in the last 10 to 15 years in England is that we are well on the way to becoming a 'classless' society. However, we have to be careful here in our definitions. Fox's research shows undoubtedly that class-consciousness is alive and well among us, because (2004, p. 406):

- Our class still determines our taste, behaviour, judgments and interactions.
- Class is not judged at all on wealth, but purely on noneconomic indicators such as speech, manners, taste and lifestyle choices.
- We have acutely sensitive on-board class radar systems.
- We deny all this in a coy squeamishness about class in public.

On the other hand, Billy Bragg celebrates the 'broadly accepted fact' (2006, p. 240) of the classless society while accepting that class-consciousness does still exist. What he means is that these days 'class is no barrier to achievement'. I am not sure I agree with his assessment. Clearly there have been enormous changes in the last 50 or so years as to who can rise to the top jobs, but nevertheless there is research which shows that the top professions still contain disproportionate numbers of public school and Oxbridge educated employees.

What interests me more, though, is that it is only since I have been working on this book and the course associated with it that I have been part of a discussion in church and among Christians about class. I am fairly certain I have never heard a sermon about our attitudes to class in this country and I can only conclude that Fox is right that we are in deep denial about our attitudes to class.

Both Paxman and Fox quote the aphorism that 'it is impossible for an Englishman [and presumably an Englishwoman] to open his mouth without making some other Englishman hate him or despise him'. Which takes us straight to the 1960s sketch featuring John Cleese, Ronnie Barker and Ronnie Corbett as embodiments of the upper, middle and lower classes, each describing their status in relation to the others. It is just as popular today, as there several versions of it available on YouTube. The fact that all three men stand in descending order of height somehow it makes it all the funnier. But is it me, or is the laughter in the background just a touch more nervous than usual canned laughter?

Fair play

Finally we meet the unique values of the English, which are as Fox describes them 'ideals – fundamental guiding principles' (2004, p. 406), and the first of which is fair play. We know of course that there are always going to be winners and losers, but we need to be sure that everyone has a fair chance to show what they can do. This applies to the whole of life, not just to sport; hence our unique love of queuing, breaking the rules of which is probably about as sinful as you can get in England.

Queuing rules did not apply in Tanzania, despite our local post office's being designed on much the same lines as the ones back home. After years of standing tall and simply holding off all comers as I tried to keep some semblance of decorum in the crush at my chosen counter, I came to visit an English post office again. It was a small suburban one with a couple of counters near the end of the shop. I went up and stood behind the person being served at the counter, there not being much of a queue. Big mistake! 'Get back and stand behind the line!' was the command from the assistant behind the counter. I wondered for a moment what line this was supposed to be – but there it was on the floor, a suitable English distance from the counter, and properly chastened I retreated behind it to wait my turn.

I also think that an extension of the fairness rule, when we apply it to ourselves, is what really gets us into action and fighting back. When we are treated unfairly and become the underdog, when our 'backs are against the wall' – that's when you begin to see what we are made of. This is surely behind the history we tell of our experiences in the Second World War. The 'Dunkirk spirit' and the reaction of Londoners and people of many other cities to the Blitz both speak of the resolve of the English when faced with overwhelming odds. Far from breaking us, the German bombing spree strengthened what may have been in other countries a very fragile resolve (Paxman, 1999, p. 86).

Courtesy

It is worth recounting here the experiment carried out by Kate Fox which defines this particular value. It is widely held that English people, if bumped into, will apologize to the person who has bumped into them (who will also probably be apologetic). So she decides to deliberately bump into people and see if this is actually the case. Apparently in about 80 per cent of cases, a proportion that changes only slightly with differences in the ethnic background of those involved, the apology comes before she makes one herself – and of course, being English, it takes her quite an effort in the first place to suppress the 'sorry!' impulse on bumping into people. Thus there is a kind of 'negative politeness' characteristic of the English, which is 'concerned with other people's need not to be intruded or imposed upon' (2004, p. 408) and which is summed up in the phrase 'sorry!' Sometimes it seems this impulse is very strong in people who almost seem to be apologizing for their very existence.

I believe it to be true that, as Fox claims, our courtesy seems to be almost entirely a matter of form – and the best example of this is the post-service handshake ritual the clergy have to go through every week on Sunday (and after most funerals and weddings too, no doubt). 'Nice sermon/service, Vicar' is a courteous greeting, but it is entirely devoid of meaning and I often suspect is covering up all sorts of other things that could or even should be said. Perhaps this rule is actually there to 'protect us from ourselves', as we wouldn't know how to give proper feedback without being unpleasant.

Modesty

This final value, of course, turns the tables on the clergyperson who has done a genuinely good job and is praised properly for it – what do you do with such a blessing? The knee-jerk response is usually 'Oh, it was nothing,' which is exactly the kind of self-deprecating, even ironic modesty we are talking about here – even if it is, when taken at face value, manifestly untrue. But even that is not a problem, as the English listener is able to effortlessly translate the 'nothing' as something quite significant. Modesty is coded in our culture.

Thus we play down our differences of wealth, intelligence, status and class with what Fox calls 'polite egalitarianism'. Modesty can therefore easily become competitive in a downwardly mobile sort of way – another temptation, in my experience, during meetings of clergy: 'My lot is worse than your lot.' This brings to mind immediately the famous Monty Python 'Four Yorkshiremen' sketch. Here the four self-made men who have clearly 'pulled themselves up by their bootstraps' compete after a good dinner to explain how tough it was for them when they were young.

So there it is – a description of the culture of Englishness. We have travelled a fairly long and winding road to reach this point, but I do believe we have a description we can work with and lay alongside our faith. Perhaps more importantly, as we shall see in the next chapter, we have identified key English metaphors and sayings which are unique to our culture. We can therefore enter into our culture and engage with it through them.

We shall not however entirely leave history and myth behind, because in Chapter 4 I want to try and combine what we have learnt from anthropology with a foundational English story with a long life – that of Robin Hood.

3

Doing inculturation in England

The question I address in this chapter, given what we have discovered so far about the importance of the integration of our faith and culture and about that culture itself – Englishness – is how can we 'do' inculturation? Especially when we are inside it and therefore unaware of it. We can take it for granted by now, I hope, that there are many ways of 'doing' inculturation in any culture, but we have chosen a particular cultural anthropology approach in this book.

At this point I should declare another of my passions. As well as crossing cultures I am also drawn to the power of adult theological education to change individuals and the church community. That was one of the reasons I travelled to Tanzania to develop a theological education programme there. So what I hope to propose in this chapter is an educational approach to doing inculturation in England, the product of which is the short course that is available alongside this book. The course is simply one intervention that could be made when thinking about integrating faith and culture; I hope others will broaden what might be possible in the future, as I shall suggest in Chapter 6.

In this chapter I shall begin by addressing how we can come to know and understand our own culture – how we can 'learn' it in the sense of becoming aware of what is there and working with it. To do this we will have to think carefully about how we come to know and understand the worlds we live in and delve into the realm of education and learning – especially how adults learn. I will examine different approaches to learning and decide on one particular imaginative approach that will be the foundation for the proposed educational course. I will then explain that course, and particularly the way in which it uses six distinctive English sayings or proverbs as jumping-off points for its theological reflection.

But first let us take a step further back from learning itself and discuss epistemology – which is a term used by philosophers for talking about how we know what we know. Epistemology is about knowledge and the processes we need to discover new things. It is therefore the basis for thinking about learning and education. It is also associated with (here comes another long word that professional theologians use a lot) hermeneutics, or the art/science of interpretation. Hermeneutics deals with the question of developing meaning from texts – but not just from written texts. Any of the artefacts that make up culture convey meaning, and hermeneutics is about working out how best to discover that meaning. It is therefore intimately associated with culture.

How do we 'know' and how do we interpret?
Epistemology and hermeneutics

We need to go back to the Greek philosopher Aristotle to start this discussion. Aristotle's classical epistemology divided knowledge into three types – theoretical, practical and productive, or to use the original Greek terms, *theoria, praxis* and *poiesis.*

The *theoria* way of knowing for Aristotle is about stepping back and thinking; it is 'the quest for truth by a contemplative/reflective/non-engaged process' (Groome, 1980, p. 153). It is an end in itself – the pursuit of truth for its own sake. It proceeds via *episteme* (which is the origin of the word epistemology), knowing the good, true and beautiful; it is the 'highest form of human activity' (Smith, 1999) and leads to *sophia* or wisdom and pure human fulfilment. The problem is that it is disembodied – it is about pure thought; it is cognitive, happening only in the head, but not affective, involving the emotions; and neither does it necessarily need to end in any action. It is an end in itself.

Praxis knowing for Aristotle is a means to the ordering of society, it is about ethical behaviour and politics – judgment and discernment. It begins with a question or a situation and proceeds via *phronesis* or practical wisdom. The end or goal is to further human well-being and it is therefore an unfinished process. It is important to understand *praxis* not simply as 'practice' – doing stuff – action (Thiselton, 1992, p. 413), i.e. the putting of 'theory' into practice. We will return to this issue in a moment.

Poiesis knowing is the means by which artefacts can be manufactured, but it also utilizes creativity and so extends to the creative arts, including architecture, poetry, drama, dance and music. Its starting point is an idea or pattern and it proceeds via the *techne* or skill of the artisan or artist.

Thomas Groome, an American educationalist, has traced the process by which these three ways of knowing were combined in Aristotle and among later philosophers and theologians in the Western tradition such that they were understood in a hierarchy. *Theoria* became the ultimate way to gain wisdom (to learn, in effect) and was elevated above the other ways of knowing, to such an extent that they almost disappeared from the Western mind. It is worth quoting Groome here: 'From the Neoplatonists onward Western education was generally understood as the imparting of theoretical knowledge (i.e. from outside lived experience) which would be applied to practice. *Praxis* as a reliable way of knowing had been lost to Western philosophy' (1980, p. 160).

We are probably familiar with this process, as it has affected all of us – particularly if we went to school before somewhere around the 1980s. For example, the model of learning and knowing that the Church used to train its ministers until very recently was this theory–practice one. Until the mid-nineteenth century all Church of England clergy were required to study at Oxford or Cambridge, and even when theological colleges were developed, the courses remained theory-laden and the educational model a 'front-loaded' one. The theory imbibed at college was presumably then meant to be expended over the lifetime of the minister in 'practice'. More often than is good, an examination of a clergyperson's bookshelves will reveal quickly when he or she studied theology.

In addition, in the period of the Enlightenment the importance of distinguishing between facts and values or beliefs was emphasized. It was taken as read that science and rational thought could provide objective facts that could not be disputed – it was an era when certainty was pursued with vigour in many quarters. Such certainty, as Lesslie Newbigin has pointed out (1995), was however very dangerous, leading to the nihilism of Nietzsche and the eugenics and worse of the Nazis.

Praxis knowing and learning and the *phronesis* or practical wisdom that goes alongside it has been recovered, thankfully, via several philosophers of knowledge – such as Hegel and Karl Marx in the nineteenth century and Jürgen Habermas and Hans-Georg Gadamer in the twentieth – although in the process its definition changed in emphasis from what Aristotle would have understood.

Anthony Thiselton claims indeed (1992, p. 314) that the work of Hans-Georg Gadamer (1989) stands as a paradigm shift in epistemology and hermeneutics – or in other words a fundamental change in how we know and interpret the world. Gadamer rejects the reductionism of the modernist era in working solely with the scientific *method* of Enlightenment rationalism – that is, only dealing with what is observable and measurable but which then becomes universally true and applicable. He is therefore able to hold together the universal and the particular in a new way (Thiselton, 1992, p. 6):

> Gadamer urges the importance of the particular case within human life. We approach questions of knowledge ... from within horizons already bounded by our finite situatedness within the flow of history. But it is possible for these finite and historically conditioned horizons to be enlarged, and to expand.

In Gadamer's thought, then, lies the seed of a recovery of the importance of the particular in the West that has occurred in the years following his work. An excellent example of this is the recent development of interest in localness exemplified by the UK charity Common Ground (<www.commonground.org.uk>) and its publication in 2006 of *England in Particular: A Celebration* of the Commonplace, the Local, the Vernacular and the Distinctive (Clifford and King, 2006). A massive and comprehensive work, it covers in the style of a dictionary a huge range of subjects from crop circles to wassailing.

It might be worth thinking about the application of Gadamer's work a bit further in relation to reading the texts of the Bible. For example, when we read 'the Lord is my Shepherd' or 'I am the good Shepherd' (Ps. 23 and John's Gospel), what do we think that statement means? We have to assume first of all that the word for shepherd in Hebrew, Greek and English means much the same thing – someone who looks after sheep for a living. So there is some kind of universal applicability of the text.

Further thought though will reveal that first-century Palestinian shepherds probably did their shepherding in very different ways from twenty-first century English ones – they didn't use dogs and certainly didn't have access to quad bikes! So, in order to understand the text fully, we have enter the first-century shepherding world (or horizon, as it is known in hermeneutics) to relate the text fully to our own world or horizon. If we do this we learn that Palestinian shepherds (then and, interestingly, even today) lead their sheep in front rather than driving them from behind, which expands our horizons of meaning and knowing when relating the text to our understanding of it. Can you see then how the universal and particular are combined in this theory of the 'two horizons', to use Thiselton's phrase in the title of one of his best-known works (1980)?

No one can escape their own horizons – neither the writer of John's Gospel nor we who read it today. In order for the creative enlargement or *fusion* of horizons, as it is known technically, to occur, our horizons as 'readers' (or interpreters) are therefore required to come into contact with 'text' which is other. So if we as English people want to understand our own horizon and even to expand it then we shall have to proceed along these lines.

Thiselton goes on to apply Gadamer's insights to theology and the Christian faith. The tension between the universal and the particular reminds us of the discussion about the concept of translatability which I outlined in Chapter 1. Christianity's universal element is that it has a proper continuity in *any* culture. There are no 'privileged perspectives' (Jasper, 2004, p. 108) in Gadamer's thought, that is, there is not a single period or text that can reign over all others – so nineteenth-century English missionary Christianity is not the touchstone for how we live out our faith today and John 3.16 remains one text among many. No, the universal (not *universalizing*) element – remember Gorringe's point about 'false universals' in Chapter 1 – is that interpretation is possible in each concrete context or particular case. Gadamer in this way stands at the boundary of modern and post-modern thought (Thiselton, 1992, p. 314), emphasizing both traditional universality and radical contextuality. This brings us to an important conclusion, that '*all reality is hermeneutical*'. That is, all that we meet in life, including the culture we find ourselves part of, requires interpretation.

Gadamer's thought is complex, but he uses a simple illustration as to how people may apprehend truth and expand their horizons (1989, pp. 101ff). He introduces the concept of 'play'. The game has to be entered into fully by the player such that it becomes a 'world' of its own. This world has to be taken absolutely seriously and its rules adhered to faithfully. If these elements are in place the participant in the game can discover it as a 'sphere of disclosure' (Jasper, 2004). Hermeneutics begins, according to Thiselton, by 'asking what it is to stand in the shoes of the other and to listen in openness' (1992, p. 28). Entering into another 'world' in this way is important for us and is an idea we shall return to later in the chapter.

We have seen how Gadamer holds the universal and particular in tension while searching for and believing in the possibility of a true interpretation of every 'text'. So that in the interaction of text and understanding, particular and universal, there is no fixed character to either element – the one interprets the other, which can then return to its source and the whole thing can start again. Thus interpretation is not a linear process 'along a trajectory from ignorance to understanding via the medium of the text' (Jasper, 2004, p. 21). Rather, interpretation and understanding proceeds in a circle or spiral; the issue is not how we get out of it or make it cease its endless process, if that were indeed possible – but 'how we get in' in the first place (2004, p. 21, following Heidegger).

Other thinkers took up the issues raised by Gadamer in the twentieth century and so his work developed in several directions. Two of these directions are relevant for us and they relate to the work of Jürgen Habermas (1978) and Paul Ricoeur (1970, 1981).

Socio-critical hermeneutics and the work of Paulo Freire

Jürgen Habermas created what is called a socio-critical hermeneutics, which 'seeks to unmask uses of texts which serve self-interests or the interests of dominating power structures' (Thiselton, 1992, p. 6). Habermas was part of the neo-Marxist Frankfurt School in Germany and their socio-critical hermeneutics is the source of the theologies that might be familiar to some readers as liberation theologies. Liberation theologies can operate in many different, usually marginalized contexts, such as among the poor in Latin America, Black people in the USA and women, as in feminist and womanist theologies. Their thought is an 'emancipatory critique' which 'reaches beyond horizons of particular persons or communities' (1992, p. 7).

We are now ready to return to the idea of *praxis* as a way of knowing and learning. It was the Brazilian educationalist Paulo Freire (1972) who championed the notion of *praxis*, based on these socio-critical hermeneutics, and turned it into a cyclical educational methodology which addressed key issues in the lives of those he was working with.

In Freire we find a fundamental shift – or 'epistemological break', to use the words of the liberation theologians – in the process of education, one which took the concrete situation of the poor seriously. He asks the critical question: 'why are we in this situation [of oppression]?' An essentially rationalist 'from theory to practice' approach will not help answer this question since it can hardly recognize the question as a question. This is why the rationalist approach has been criticized from many perspectives, not least in that it produces a 'thin, one-dimensional' meaning that can be accused of leading to (and being productive of) Western hegemonic colonialism (Brueggemann, 2005). Freire described it educationally as 'banking' education, where the teacher holds all the information and therefore the power. The teacher transfers selected information from the bank to the students – which changes nothing about their concrete situation.

Freire thus introduced the question of power relations into the educational process and its outcome; for him that outcome is political action to transform society emerging from reflection on experience. *Praxis* education for Freire is a dialectic between action and reflection which enables students to become aware of their concrete, historical situation of being oppressed by the powerful. He calls this process *conscientization.*

Freire proved *praxis* to be a very powerful educational method-ology as he was able to teach illiterate peasants to read and write within six weeks and in the process give them political awareness about their own experience of oppression.

Freire's approach has changed the way learning and teaching proceeds, but he was not without his critics. There is a great deal of literature dealing positively and critically with his work (for an overview of two different approaches see Johns, 1993 and Astley, 1994). Despite any limitations of Freire's work, it does form the basis today for many secular approaches to life-long learning and professional development which move beyond the filling-up of students with theory in initial training in order to expend the theory in professional practice. (See Mezirow and associates (1990) and Schön (1991).)

In theology this cyclical methodology has resulted in the championing of the so-called 'pastoral cycle' by, for instance, Laurie Green (1990). Some readers may be familiar with this approach, which despite being an inevitable over-simplification of the way theological reflection proceeds, clearly has its uses in uncovering and unmasking difficulties and issues for Christians, particularly at the grass roots of the Church. It follows the cycle: experience – reflection on that experience – engaging with the tradition – planning for action to develop a new experience – and therefore beginning again.

The question for us, though, is how useful this method might be in the project of inculturation in England. My issue with it as an approach is that it remains a somewhat rationalist and critical method, and in practice a confrontational one. In my experience people do not like being confronted with their own culture – just think of the person who comes fresh to a new country and culture and begins telling the inhabitants what is wrong with the way they go about things. The critic may of course be right, but he or she cannot be heard. For an insider, to be confronted in this way by an outsider is really too painful to take.

Let me offer a biblical example. Think about the prophet Nathan confronting King David (2 Sam. 12) with the sin of the murder of Uriah the Hittite after his adultery with Uriah's wife, Bathsheba. How is he going to go about what is a very delicate and sensitive task? Nathan could have tried a 'theory to practice' approach and simply restated the sixth and seventh command-ments to his king. But this was the king we are talking about. Such an approach would undoubtedly have led to a denial (we are still familiar with the importance among the powerful of developing 'plausible deniability' scenarios) and probably to considerable danger for Nathan.

Nathan was no doubt unaware of the pastoral cycle, but we can try and imagine how he might have attempted to employ it. 'So, King David, let us reflect on your experience here. Why are we in this situation?' Once again it is difficult to see how this approach, even if it had been available to Nathan, would have got past David's inability to see the world from any perspective other than his own as the powerful king of the whole nation.

So what does Nathan do? He employs the imagination, what could be called the 'back door' into David's heart and mind. He tells a story, a parable that so engages David's mind and emotions that he cannot escape the accusation when it comes: 'You are the man!' And this gives us a clue to getting inside the 'hearts and minds' of the English and their culture.

Paul Ricoeur and the hermeneutics of the imagination

In Chapter 1 we saw how inculturation is about both entering into and becoming part of a culture (as Christ did in the incarnation), as well as transforming it according to the 'gospel'. We now turn to a second branch of hermeneutics that grew from Gadamer's initial work – the branch developed by Paul Ricoeur. In a direct connection with the double movement in inculturation, I believe, we have Ricoeur's definition of hermeneutics (1970, p. 27): 'Hermeneutics seems to me to be animated by this double motivation: willingness to suspect, willingness to listen; vow of rigor, vow of obedience.'

In practice this means that the interpreter must be aware of the temptation to project his or her own constructs, culture and ideas on to texts so that they are no longer 'other'. This is exactly why it is so difficult to examine our own culture from within its horizons: we simply see everything else through the lenses provided by our culture. What do we do then? Rather we should be listening in openness to symbol, story and metaphor, which will allow for creative newness to occur 'in front of the text' (Ricoeur, 1981, p. 143; Bartholomew, 2005). Ricoeur's is a hermeneutics of both suspicion and retrieval (Thiselton, 1992, p. 344).

Craig Bartholomew explicitly connects Ricoeur's hermeneutics with culture because hermeneutics is essentially about how we understand 'world' (2005, p. 139), by which he means, I think, a kind of comprehensive world-view out of which we know now that our specific cultures emerge. This relates to the work of the practical theologian Terry Veling (2005), who understands interpretation to be about asking the question 'can I move from the world I currently inhabit to a new world that I *could* inhabit?' (2005, p. 47, his italics).

Graham, Walton and Ward (2005) also underline the importance of using imagination and therefore metaphor in this method. Following Ricoeur, they state that metaphors bring together what were previously distinct terms into a new conjunction, so that 'metaphor shatters not only the previous structure of our language, but also the previous structures of what we call reality' (2005, p. 64).

Thus, through metaphor we receive a 'new way of being in the world' which gives metaphor (and consequently literary text) – according to Graham, Walton and Ward, quoting Rowan Williams – a *revelatory* function (2005, p. 65): 'it [revelation] displays a possible world, a reality in which my human reality can find itself, and inviting me into its world the text breaks open and extends my possibilities.'

This dynamic and dialectical understanding of revelation can lead to the human person's not being required to submit to a pre-scribed truth (e.g. 'King David, just listen to the commandments as handed down to us') but rather to his or her imagination being called upon to open itself to new possibilities. This is also how the parables of Jesus and his miraculous actions work in the Gospels. An imaginative and metaphorical approach is therefore at the very least related to the inculturation task.

An imaginative approach to inculturation work

During the research that was the starting point for this work, I studied in depth the Education for Ministry (EFM) course, the theoretical background to which is described in some detail in the book *The Art of Theological Reflection* (Killen and De Beer, 1994).

This is not the place to go into a full description of the course and its theoretical background, although I will outline it further in a moment (see also <www.efm-uk.org.uk> and Rooms, 2010 for further details if you are interested). What is important to note for our purposes is that although the method of theological reflection employed in the course has elements of cyclical hermeneutics and the pastoral cycle contained within it, at the heart of it is the theological examination of a metaphor or saying.

The basic idea is this: that metaphors and parables create a world. We have seen this proposition put forward several times in this chapter in different ways. Such a world can be entered into, even lived within, for a while in the participant's imagination. In this way the subject can have a look around and ask questions of the imaginary (but real and related) world. If the questions are framed in a certain way they can become theological (without the questioner necessarily realizing that he or she is asking theological questions!). Thus the world created by the metaphor becomes a reality in the consciousness of the learner, but in a way which can be examined critically without the same level of threat provided by the other approaches we have looked at – at least initially.

The genius of utilizing the imagination is that it offers us a way of helping individuals to cross the boundary of their own culture without actually physically leaving it. I noted in Chapter 1 that my own journey into crossing cultures began when I travelled outside the country of my birth for the first time. Not everyone can do that, and so using the imagination in this way enables people to step out of or rise above their own culture for a while before returning to it, hopefully, enlightened and conscientized about it. What they don't need to do is buy an aeroplane ticket and fly somewhere else.

How does this idea work in practice? At the end of Chapter 2 I described the ten characteristics of Kate Fox's 'cultural English genome' and noted how some kind of saying or proverb was associated with almost all of them. We also know from the previous chapter that the culture of a people can be encapsulated by their proverbs and sayings. So at this point we are ready for a key move in our study of Englishness and faith. We can bring together the theological reflection method described by Killen and De Beer, and utilized in the EFM course, with Fox's English characteristics and their associated sayings and proverbs. If we choose carefully, we can identify some of these universal English metaphors and aphorisms as starting points for the theological reflection that will enable us to place Englishness in dialogue with the gospel. We can create English 'worlds' from them to be examined theologically.

The best example of this is the saying 'An Englishman's home is his castle.' While there is evidence that, historically, this truism does not have a very long tradition in England,[1] it has come to encapsulate for us the English love of privacy driven by some deep need for refuge from external pressures and people. It even gets pride of place (if in a rather clunky way) in a key speech by Russell Crowe in the Hollywood blockbuster film *Robin Hood* (2010), which we shall be looking at in more detail in the next chapter.

At the heart of the proverb is a metaphor – the idea that for the English home is *like* a castle. So we invite people to enter a world that is wholly characterized by that idea and ask them questions about it. We can ask those somewhat disguised theological questions we referred to earlier that might revolve around

- creation (what is this world like, how does it feel?);
- incarnation (what is it like to truly dwell in this world and what 'gospel' does it evoke – what is good and true about it?);
- death and resurrection (what deaths, if any, are required in this world to transform it into a better world, what might need to be let go of?);
- the eschaton (what is the best possible picture we could have of this world, or what would be a reason for a party in it?).

In Killen and De Beer's method of doing theological reflection this is not the end of the interaction. Once the cultural metaphor has been examined, participants choose (or can be given) a short piece of Scripture (a verse, a few words or a phrase) or a story from the tradition to lay alongside the metaphor, one that is evoked by it or resonates with it.

So, for instance, when I used the home/castle metaphor with certain groups, they came up with interesting scriptural references such as Jeremiah 29.5, 'Build houses and live in them' (REB), and John 20.19, 'when the doors were locked [in the upper room]' (my translation). These are treated in the same way as the initial metaphor – i.e. it is assumed that the phrase

---

[1] As we shall see, it was popularized in Charles Dickens's *Great Expectations* in the nineteenth century.

creates another 'world' that can be entered into. With the example given above, participants can live in the upper room with its locked doors after the resurrection and examine that space in their imaginations.

This imaginative reflection offers further critique of the starting metaphor as the two sets of questions and answers relating to the two worlds are laid alongside each other and compared and contrasted. From this point on (and sometimes even earlier), the learners gain and share *insights*; that is, new meaning and understanding arise for those taking part. Then participants are asked what incidents from their lives the reflection evokes in them and they tell these stories as appropriate. Next they take up 'positions' where they give a brief statement of what they believe at the end of the reflection. Finally, they are asked what action they will undertake as a result of what has happened and where they now stand. Readers from this point on could refer usefully to the course published with this book for an understanding of the process.

A reflection such as the one using home/castle is hard work, but given around one and a half to two hours it can be very fruitful. For the course I have created six such studies which use much the same method each time. If a reflection is used once per week, then with a maximum of six reflections the course becomes a short and manageable way of engaging anyone with the interaction of Englishness and faith. Since piloting the course I have added an optional seventh session which reviews the course and asks what the future implications of the studies are for the participants and the community they belong to.

This means that we are looking for six sayings or proverbs that characterize Englishness. I name the six sayings below and then explain how we get to them from Kate Fox's original ten characteristics:

1 Moderation: 'Don't rock the boat'
2 Humorous moaning: 'Typical!'
3 Privacy: 'An Englishman's home is his castle'

4 Fair play: 'Well, to be fair . . .'
5 Class: 'I know my place'
6 Courtesy: 'Sorry!'

I think we can distil Fox's initial ten English characteristics down to six, since some of them overlap in and between the three groups of reflexes, outlooks and values, and one ('social dis-ease') holds them all together. Moderation, fair play, class and courtesy are all directly present among the six reflections. 'Social dis-ease' as the catch-all is dealt with via privacy; humour and Eeyorishness are combined in the second reflection on humorous moaning; and modesty is combined with courtesy in the saying 'Sorry!' The only characteristic I do not really touch on is empiricism, and while we could probably find a metaphor to go with it ('the proof of the pudding . . .'), it would make the course longer than necessary.

Having spent some time looking at 'An Englishman's home is his castle', I shall explain a bit more about each of the other sayings. Before I do, though, I should also remark that these proverbs and sayings are often *multivalent* – they have a range of meanings which can only be fully explored through the theological microscope we put them under in the course.

'Don't rock the boat'

Perhaps being a nation surrounded by the sea as well as one that built its empire on seafaring has helped this saying take hold among us. The idea is a simple one: boats rely on stability and most people if asked would not want to die by drowning, so keeping your boat 'on an even keel', to put it another way, is vitally important. There is something inherently conservative about us, the English, which keeps us in the middle of the boat, not wanting to risk unbalancing it by moving to the edge. Yet the saying needs to be questioned, since a boat that is not rocking at all is hardly going anywhere. An issue that arises in relation to gospel themes might be: if moderation is so important to us, how does change and transformation happen in England?

'Typical!'

I referred in Chapter 2 to the source of this national catchphrase and its frequent use when things seem inevitably to go wrong. Just today I decided to take my car to the garage to deal with a very annoying high-pitched squeal that had been there the weekend before last. I found myself explaining to the mechanic that of course (typical!) it had disappeared now, but could he have a look at it anyway? Enough said – but I hope the reflection will help us to think about a world that is wholly characterized by this attitude and therefore what might be the benefits or otherwise of our humorous moaning.

'Well, to be fair . . .'

In her research Kate Fox hears a myriad of expressions relating to fairness; as well as our chosen phrase, there is also 'In all fairness . . .'; 'given a fair chance'; 'come on, it's only fair'; 'fair's fair'; 'fair enough'; 'firm but fair'; 'fair and square'; 'it's a fair cop' (2004, p. 407).

Given this enormous variety of ways of saying what seems like essentially the same thing, you would think that the concept of fairness and fair play would be simple. However, it became clear in choosing the actual phrase to work with on this reflection that there are subtle nuances hidden away in each particular saying. So 'Well, to be fair . . .' anticipates that balancing of both sides of an argument that is so important to the English and which I wanted to capture here.

'I know my place'

It is worth telling the story of how I came to this phrase, one which sums up the English attitude to class. In preparation for writing this book and the course that comes with it, I piloted the educational programme with some local groups. On the first run-through I shared my difficulty about finding the right phrase for the class reflection in Week 5. I thought that a group might in general be able to decide whether it looked up the social scale or down, and so could choose an appropriate phrase for either option. But then I realized that most groups, wherever they really were on the scale, would probably say they were somewhere in the middle and looked *both* ways.

This was the dilemma, until I was rescued the week before the session. One of the participants offered the idea of using the famous 1960s sketch with John Cleese, Ronnie Barker and Ronnie Corbett that I referred to in Chapter 2. The sketch is actually called 'I Know My Place', as this is the phrase Ronnie Corbett, playing the working-class man, uses repeatedly as the refrain of the piece. So we had found the right saying to work with – when we are honest with ourselves we all really do know our place.

'Sorry!'

We have already noted Kate Fox's experiment in bumping into other people, the source of this saying which is so short but means so much. It begins so many sentences and interactions in English life that it is definitely worth a reflection of its own.

One example that comes to mind is the board game simply titled Sorry!. As I remember it, this is a version of Ludo that allows a player to announce a rather hypocritical 'sorry!' as his or her opponents are bumped off the board and back to the start. Or think of the title of the popular Radio Four game show *I'm Sorry I Haven't a Clue!*. Why would we need to be sorry for our ignorance? But we are.

Where are we now?

Up to this point I have described how, theologically, culture and faith interact through the concept of inculturation. A description of English culture has been offered from serious anthropological and semiotic research. In this chapter we have reviewed several possible methods for engaging English people with their own culture in a theological way, from the standpoint of the Christian faith. An imaginative method that employs metaphor and sayings has been chosen as the vehicle for bringing faith and English culture together through six definitive English sayings.

A reflective study course is available for use with small groups to explore Englishness and the gospel.

The next chapter both continues this theme and stands alone of itself. We shall be examining in detail the Robin Hood legends, quintessentially English stories that have grown up and lived over the centuries in the imagination of English people. Hopefully this will give us further clues as to the nature of an interaction between Englishness and faith which will be explored fully in Chapter 5, before I finally look at the implications of our study for mission in England today in Chapter 6.

4

Robin Hood – a foundational English story

'*In the heart of England lives a legend.*'

When the BBC ran a Robin Hood TV series in the middle 'noughties', the above slogan was prominently displayed on the opening credits of every episode. I believe the statement to be true in both senses in which it can be taken. The story of Robin Hood continues to live in the imaginations of the English, but also internationally via Hollywood, which, as I write, has just produced another version (*Robin Hood*, Universal Pictures, 2010). Deeper than this though, the legend lives in the hearts of the English; it describes in story form something about our foundational beliefs and values that no book on Englishness and Christianity can ignore. We will explore it at some depth in this chapter as we allow it to interact with Kate Fox's characteristics of the English genome, considered in Chapter 2, and the place of the gospel in England.

There are three main reasons for exploring the fruitfulness of the Robin Hood legend in this book. It is first of all an enduring narrative which has survived over many centuries and does not seem to lose its appeal – in fact it has been strengthened globally since we entered the televisual/cinematic age. The legend has metamorphosed through several different versions, as we shall see, but fundamentally it endures.

Second, the stories have an interesting relationship with the Christian faith. Ostensibly, on the surface at least, there is not only an historical antagonism between Robin Hood and the Church within the stories themselves, but also hostility from the Church towards the legend and the practices associated with it. In the earliest written reference to Robin Hood, dating from the late 1370s, William Langland in his moral satire *Piers Plowman* depicts a priest representing Sloth who knows the stories of Robin Hood but not the Lord's Prayer (Knight, 2003, p. 3). Bishop Hugh Latimer in the sixteenth century inveighs against the people celebrating 'Robyn hoodes day' in May when they should be in church (2003, p. 4).

Nevertheless it is also a Christian story, despite the ambivalence of the official Church – Julian Barnes sums it up as he presents it in a key part of his novel *England, England* (1998). Barnes describes the Robin Hood legend thus (1998, p. 146), and explains the reason it is given high priority in the English theme park created by entrepreneur Sir Jack Pitman:

> Robin Hood and his Merrie Men. Riding through the glen. Stole from the rich, gave to the poor. Robin Hood, Robin Hood. A primal myth; better still a primal English myth. One of freedom and rebellion – justified rebellion of course. Wise, if *ad hoc*, principles of taxation and redistribution of income. Individualism deployed to temper the excesses of the free market. The brotherhood of man. A Christian myth, too, despite certain anti-clerical features. The pastoral monastery of Sherwood Forest. The triumph of the virtuous yet seemingly outgunned over the epitomic robber baron.

Versions of the Robin Hood stories occur and have been celebrated as far north as Scotland and in many parts of the South of England, while a Yorkshire' setting in Barnsdale is not discounted. Yet our final point in focusing on Robin Hood is that the story has settled in Nottinghamshire in the East Midlands, something I believe is significant for England as a whole.[1]

---

[1] I should declare an interest at this point. I have lived a significant part of my life in Nottinghamshire and currently do so, even to the extent that fortuitously, even providentially, I have a postal address of 'Robin Hood Chase'! My study of Robin Hood is, I hope, a contribution to an emerging English contextual theology, a discipline in which I have a long-standing interest.

Most of us would be familiar with the myth as summarized by Julian Barnes; however this is just the most recent version of it. Before we can assess the overall value of the stories for our project, we must understand the development of the myth over the centuries from its earliest period. Along the way we can point out the resonances with core English reflexes, outlooks and values as we have identified them with Kate Fox's work. Once that is complete we can summarize how Robin Hood is a foundational story for the English and begin to think about its relationship to the gospel.

The Robin Hood literary scholar Stephen Knight elucidates four periods of the development of the myth (2003):

1 'Bold Robin Hood' – the pre-Reformation period
2 'Robert, Earl of Huntingdon' – the post-Reformation period
3 'Robin Hood Esquire' – late eighteenth and nineteenth century
4 'Robin of Hollywood' – twentieth century and beyond.

There is of course probably some kind of fifth period preceding (1) when the oral tradition begins, before the first written reference in *Piers Plowman* and before the first stories are written down in the fifteenth century. And inevitably there is a quest for the 'historical Robin Hood'. In the 1990s, in searches in court records, there were found several references to outlaws being called 'Robehod' (Wood, 2000, p. 74), some as early as 1230 (Pollard, 2007, p. 5), although whether this is the same effect as someone writing 'Mickey Mouse' in a visitor's book – in other words it's a pseudonym – or whether men genuinely were given the name Robin Hood is difficult to tell at this distance. The general consensus of scholarship is that it is enormously difficult to state with any certainty whether there was an historical figure who bore much resemblance to the outlaw we now know and love. There is certainly a bit more evidence for the historical Jesus!

I shall now take each of these periods in turn in order to build up a picture of how the legend grew, developed and changed. We will spend more time and effort on the earlier periods as I think these are the more important, formative ones. Recent versions are both more familiar to us and draw on and remix

75

the preceding stories. They are therefore more easily interpreted in the light of what has gone before.

The pre-Reformation era

This period is important for a couple of reasons. First, it is where the myth was recorded in written form for the first time; second, the versions of the stories to which it gives rise are perhaps the least familiar to us, being the most distant in time.

The key work on this period, by A. J. Pollard (2007), thoroughly explores all aspects of the early written myths. The period begins in the fifteenth century and continues into the early sixteenth, during which the stories were spoken and sung and then written down. As late and very late medieval texts (Pollard, 2007, p. x), they tell us mostly about their own period and only in 'collective memory' about any earlier period.

Pollard thinks that there were originally about eight stories, all of which were written down by around 1500. Of course there may have been many more oral versions, but these are the ones that survive. They are stories built around the 'stock character' of Robin Hood and his few friends, the king and basic enemies such as the Sheriff. They are a little bit like the stories in modern-day comics where the characters appear and reappear and are recycled each week. These were very popular stories, as commentators remarked at the time, easily 'outselling' those about other, less popular heroes of the period (2007, p. 3).

Some elements in these stories have survived throughout the whole trajectory of the legends down the centuries. Robin is an outlaw. His companions are the Merry Men – Little John, Will Scarlet and Much the Miller's Son. They live and hide out in Sherwood Forest. They poach the king's deer and rob travellers in the Forest, but in a 'pleasant' way, inviting them to eat with the band first. They are skilful archers – especially Robin. Some action, particularly archery contests, takes place in Nottingham, and Robin's arch-enemy is the Sheriff. Robin does not like monks – especially Benedictines. He remains loyal to the king.

In these early stories we immediately note several characteristic English themes. There is humour among the Merry Men, perhaps exemplified by the name given to Little John. We perhaps do not notice the reversal implied by the name as we are so used to this kind of understated epithet. Of course you would give any huge man called John the nickname 'little'. There is courtesy too, and humour, contained within the idea of inviting those you rob to have a meal with you first – and not a little hypocrisy in the process.

There are, however, major differences between these early stories and those more familiar to us. Friar Tuck makes only a peripheral entrance in a play version of one of the stories. There is no Maid Marian, although Robin is devoted to the Virgin Mary. Robin 'robs from the undeserving and helps the deserving, but he does not rob from the rich and give to the poor' (Pollard, 2007, p. 4). The king is an Edward, not Richard I – although which Edward up to 1340 is unclear (2007, p. 187). And Robin is a plain yeoman – of which more in a moment.

In the fifteenth century five of the stories in circulation were 'harmonized' into one, which then gained wide circulation and survives as the *Gest of Robyn Hode*. The five stories deal successively with a knight down on his luck rescued by Robin; with Robin and the Sheriff in Nottingham; with Little John and the Sheriff; with Robin's entering the king's court, which he then gives up to return to his former life in the greenwood; and finally with Robin's death, betrayed at the hands of a prioress in Yorkshire.

While the *Gest* is hardly a smooth harmonization of the different stories, Pollard states that it 'is clearly recognizable as the basis of all later versions' (2007, p. 6). It was possibly composed as early as 1400, although the earliest surviving copy dates from 1492. The compiler is unknown. There are three other stories in existence that were not incorporated in the *Gest* and Pollard also deals with these. *Robin Hood and the Monk* involves Little John's falling out with Robin but later being restored. *Robin Hood and the Potter* entails Robin's taking a potter's disguise and bringing about more trouble for the Sheriff in Nottingham, while the final story, *Guy of Gisborne*, features the appearance of the eponymous character, who is killed at the end along with the Sheriff. In the stories, according to Pollard (2007, p. 12), Robin is not portrayed in a single fashion but in several different ways – as a restorer of justice, as a cold-blooded killer, as courteous and high-minded and as a trickster.

The stories are written in rhyme and may have been chanted or recited. There is also a whole genre of plays that were performed particularly in May and June at the May Games in villages and towns throughout the country, but which were later suppressed during the Reformation. Pollard suggests that the audience for the *Gest* and the other stories lies between the freeborn gentleman and the commoners (2007, p. 9). In other words, the stories have a wide social appeal and yet are also subversive of authority from the start. They are spoken against, as we have noted, particularly by church authorities.

It is important for our purposes to understand that Robin Hood 'became, literally, proverbial' (2007, p. 11). Thus the early fifteenth-century proverb 'many men speak of Robin Hood who never shot his bow', which I suppose is an earlier version of 'Robin Hood, Robin Hood riding through the glen . . .' (see also Knight, 2003, p. 7).

So what of the Robin Hood who is portrayed in these early stories? First of all he is a yeoman, about which there is much discussion as to the social status implied by the term. In the context of the late medieval world the current consensus is that yeomen were a kind of emerging middle class, located socially between the peasants and the gentry. Quoting Colin Richmond, Pollard associates Robin Hood with an intermediary and transitional status of 'yeomanliness', and in conclusion states that 'Robin Hood was the personification of non-gentry aspirations and of the hopes of "people of handicraft", artisan as well as husbandman, urban as well as rural' (2007, p. 31).

From the beginning, then, class-consciousness is displayed in the stories. The development of the original legends even seems to coincide with the beginnings of an emerging middle class, embodied in the yeoman order.

Even at this early stage Robin Hood emerges as an 'in-between' character in social terms. 'He is both of intermediary rank and of intermediary status. The liminal character of this situation means that Robin Hood is a hero cut for all' (2007, p. 56). So there is a proper English moderation in all this – never straying too far from the middle way.

Everyone knows that Robin Hood's domain was the greenwood – and this was so also in the fifteenth century, although Sherwood Forest in Nottinghamshire seemed to merge seamlessly into Barnsdale in Yorkshire. But this is also a mythical, imaginary place where it is always May and the trees are just coming into leaf – an Arcadia if you like, an ideal world. What is more important, however, is the fact that the action takes place 'north of the [River] Trent', so that the 'greenwood is also distant from metropolitan and southern England' (2007, p. 58). The story is never relocated from this position and I believe it could not really take place anywhere else. As an essentially subversive story it could not be located nearer the capital of England. The Trent, it seems to me, does form some kind of boundary between the north and south of the country (although the actual location of the north–south divide depends a bit on your starting point and historical period (2007, p. 67)). The kingdom of Northumbria in the very early medieval period extended to the Trent and, in the east at least, it still forms the boundary of the Northern Province of the Church of England. Nottingham, of course, with a major crossing-point of the Trent close by, was the gateway to the north.

It is also likely that these are southern stories about the north, and so drew on a stereotype of the north in the imaginary greenwood (2007, p. 64). The north was thought by southerners to be wild, uncivilized and lawless, not least thanks to the widespread citation of Jeremiah 1.14 – 'Out of the north an evil shall break forth upon all the inhabitants of the land' (KJV). This imaginary world was very far from the truth, as Pollard shows (2007, p. 68); nevertheless the 'literary convention', as it arose, of the wild north was useful for those who wanted to tell stories of the 'violent but cleansing' lives of outlaws in this period (2007,

p. 71). So the greenwood has a dual role – both as an idealized Arcadian world where it is always spring and where youth and hope can have their day, and as the place where 'raw nature represents the hard and imperfect world'. Just as autumn and winter follow spring, the Arcadian world cannot last. This is a 'subliminal dimension to what the greenwood signified' in these narratives (2007, p. 81).

These early Robin Hood stories are violent; the Sheriff and Guy of Gisborne meet violent ends. Perhaps such violence echoes the dark side of the English 'social dis-ease' described by Fox, although Pollard is clear here that violence in the pursuit of justice, arising as it does from chivalric values, is understood and allowed in medieval society (2007, p. 108). The Sheriff can be viewed as 'the personification of the malign exercise of power'. Even at this stage he is still subverting the king's just rule and is dealt with accordingly, thus 'restoring true justice'. Violence has a cleansing aspect in this world-view. Robin Hood therefore celebrates 'righteous violence to maintain true justice precisely when the officers of the law have failed' (2007, p. 109). Again we find him located between the righteous and unrighteous upholders of the law – between King and Sheriff.

This leads us immediately to another tension in the myth as it was first conceived. Robin Hood can be seen both to affirm and subvert authority – he affirms the true justice of the King against the perverted justice of the Sheriff. As Pollard notes, 'the noble robber is not therefore a social revolutionary, he seeks restorative justice, the re-establishment of things as they used to be and ought to be' (2007, p. 157).

The key tension and source of drama in the stories is held here. It is easy to see how, at one extreme, the stories could be co-opted by the establishment for their own ends, and at the other, Robin can be held to be a revolutionary about to over-throw the system. Again it depends a lot on the reader/listener's place in the system or social hierarchy – there were 'contested meanings which were being continuously negotiated'. To conclude, with Pollard, Robin is 'the personification of the loyal rebel, who by being outside the law defends the law and by being disorderly restores order' (2007, p. 182). Stephen Knight concurs: 'Deep in these ballads is an inherently antiauthoritarian idea that the powerful depend for their power on the consent and activity of ordinary people, and so ordinary people could assume those roles in a spirit of resistance, whether serious, playfully deceptive, or both at once' (2003, p. 20).

Here is another confirmation of the Englishness of the myth. Robin Hood stands in the middle ground, for moderation and fair play. If there is a political element to the stories it is this idea of the assumption of the consent of the people, which can be taken for granted most of the time – but should the powerful overstep the mark, look out! I am writing this in the middle of an election campaign, during which party leaders are acutely aware of the need to avoid any hint of triumphalism. They all remember the more than bloody nose that Neil Kinnock was given by the electorate in 1992 after seeming to assume victory at an election rally in Sheffield.

We have already pointed out that Robin Hood is a Christian myth. This too is borne out by the early stories. Robin is good and honest and embodies at least something of what it is to be truly Christian. These qualities again are in opposition to the hierarchy of the Church, especially the monks and nuns of the monasteries (but, interestingly, not really the bishops). Meanwhile Robin and his men are 'true servants of our lady' (Pollard, 2007, p. 119). Robin insists on hearing the Mass before getting down to his next deed and is devoted to the saints. Thus, Pollard believes, Robin is portrayed as a 'model of contemporary lay Christianity' who as such was part of the late medieval blurring of the 'traditional clear-cut distinction between clergy and laity'. Once again we find Robin in-between categories, this time religious ones.

This raises an important question for the English in relation to Christianity, one which we will return to in the final chapters. There is an assumption about Christian belief in England which finds expression in the refrain 'you don't need to go to church to be a Christian'. The sociologist Grace Davie[2] has often pointed

---

[2] For example see her essay 'Debate' in Wells and Coakley (eds) (2008), pp. 147–69.

out that there is a 'public utility' model of religion current in England whereby the Church, like the National Health Service, is 'free at the point of need'. The idea that Robin Hood can somehow exemplify a purer, truer Christian faith by being an outlaw outside the Church requires more reflection in relation to the Church's approach to mission in England today.

Robin Hood is not alone in the stories. There is a strong theme within them of fraternity and fellowship between Robin and the Merry Men – they are 'good fellows'. As such, they police the boundaries of what it means to be a good fellow and to be admitted or otherwise to the band of yeomen. Thus 'True fellowship, brotherhood and charity are to be found in Robin Hood's band. . . . False brotherhood is in the monastery' (2007, p. 149), where money and obesity seem to reign. Such fraternities and trade guilds were common in this period and so it is no surprise that Pollard concludes: 'The values and ideals of Robin Hood's fellowship reflect the essential communitarianism, common purpose and conviviality of late-medieval fraternities' (2007, p. 154).

A final point here brings together these themes of the lay Christian forming a fellowship of outlaws who restore justice. In the fourth story of the *Gest*, Robin joins the King's court, but only as an equal, not as a subject. After a time he grows tired of court life and returns to his former existence in the greenwood. He is ambivalent ultimately about royal authority because (2007, p. 209):

> The greenwood offers an alternative kingdom, an alternative social order, and an alternative 'popular' law. . . . The alternative *regnum* is founded on an awareness that kings never live up to their rhetoric, or reach the ideals of monarchy . . . it recognizes too that governments fail in their promise to put right the evils of the past. . . . Everything is changed and everything stays the same. Robin Hood is deeply distrustful of the exercise of power, and of people in power. In this respect the *Gest* is fundamentally subversive, for no government is to be trusted to maintain the common weal. When Robin walked on ground things were different in an alternative greenwood kingdom. But then, of course, so courteous an outlaw was never found.

I find this tremendously resonant of the Christ event and of the kingdom (or *basilea* as it is known in Greek) portrayed in the Gospels. We might add to Pollard that just as the kings never quite live up to their rhetoric, neither often does the Church. The tantalizing vision is set before us of an outlaw with a realizable alternative kingdom; Robin Hood represents that deep-seated understanding of and longing for such a kingdom among the English people.

And so here, in yet another sense, 'In the heart of England lives a legend.' Pollard states clearly that this was also the case in these early versions of the stories, where Robin could be all things to all men. Robin Hood is 'quintessentially of the middling sort' (2007, p. 213) in almost every way, as we have seen in these early versions of the stories.

The post-Reformation period

Pollard summarizes under four headings the changes that occurred to the Robin Hood legend after the Reformation (2007, p. 188):

1 Robin robs the rich to give to the poor.
2 Robin is a dispossessed Anglo-Saxon earl fighting the Norman occupation of England.
3 The Sheriff is an agent of the evil Prince John, but Robin is restored when Richard I returns from the Crusades.
4 Robin has a romantic attachment to Maid Marian.

These changes occurred due to the developing English context of the stories – 'the growth of modern class consciousness, the development of the myth of the Norman Yoke, the emergence of the Whig interpretation of the Magna Carta, and the displacement of Catholicism by Protestantism as the established religion'. Thus once again we see how the Robin Hood legend tracks almost perfectly the development of English consciousness through the major disruption which was the Reformation. Rather than destroy the story it simply moulds itself around the new situation.

Stephen Knight (2003) traces these developments as they lead up to Anthony Munday's work *The Downfall of Robert, Earle of Huntingdon*, published in 1598, where Robin becomes a legend with a beginning rather than just an end – he is the 'distressed gentleman' (2003, p. 44). The popularity and reach of the stories continued in the early Reformation period. Even Henry VIII enjoyed taking part in the plays and they were performed annually in towns and villages across the country, as we noted earlier, until the latter years of the sixteenth century. There then developed a whole set of public plays written by dramatists and performed by proper actors (2003, p. 52).

It was Munday who first introduced Robin as the noble exile in the time of Richard I and Prince John. Such a move certainly seems to gentrify the myth and reduce some of the more subversive elements of the earlier ballads, such as the *Gest*. Robin has moved up a class, gone back in time, and has more of a reason to fight those who oppose the rightful king. Some co-opting of the popularity of the myth with other concerns of the day seems to be going on here: 'this is an individualized drama for the landed gentry, not a yeoman's struggle for popular liberty' (2003, p. 54). Marian is introduced (probably her name is transposed from Mary to Marian, although this is not quite clear) and is caught in a love triangle with Robin and Prince John. The story has become much more one of national significance – not just one played out locally in Nottinghamshire and Yorkshire with occasional references to King and court.

This establishes for Knight 'a new narrative, realizing what has become a classic sequence for the gentrified outlaw: his banishment, his forest adventures, his encounter with the returned king, the outcome of the story – here tragic, but elsewhere happy' (2003, p. 61).

What is interesting for me is that this new direction takes the narrative ultimately to a dead end – several playwrights continue after Munday, concluding with Ben Jonson, who 'left the hero as little more than a good host and fine lover' (2003, p. 73) – so that 'gentrifying Robin has cut him off from the dynamic core of the outlaw story'. Robin Hood cannot be easily co-opted by the establishment without losing the impact of the story. The tension we noted earlier between the 'bold resister of authority and a mildly errant member of the ruling class' (2003, p. 83) comes into sharper focus in the post-Reformation period. It was not until the end of the century that this tension was resolved, when it became possible to combine Robin the 'distressed aristocrat' with Robin the 'energetic . . . social bandit' once again.

The late eighteenth and nineteenth century

Knight accords the scholar and radical Joseph Ritson prime responsibility for rescuing Robin Hood from genteel obscurity in the late eighteenth century. Ritson does this by writing a 'literary life' – a genre that became popular in this period (2003, p. 96). It is no coincidence that with the Enlightenment comes an interest in the so-called 'history' of Robin Hood. As Knight notes about the effect of this period, 'the myth had become biography'. By combining the earlier stories with the life of Robin as it was then understood, Ritson 'brought together the yeoman and the lord', outlining a hero who was undeniably gentrified but also 'memorable, exciting, bold, and adventurous'. In doing this, Ritson expresses his own somewhat complex radicalism, in that he too 'sees no contradiction in the cause of the people being led by someone from another class' (2003, p. 98). From this point onwards in the narrative tradition we recognize that Robin can be lord *and* trickster, as well as bold outlaw with noble blood, but nevertheless class is still a driver of the story.

Interestingly the Luddites, active in Nottinghamshire during the period 1811–16, distanced themselves from Robin Hood while owning his base in 'Sherwood Forest' (2003, p. 98). The radical direct action of the disaffected of this period does not find that much in common with the outlaw hero.

In a crucial period for the development of the myth, the legend is reconstructed in 1818–19 around the 'ideals of national identity, masculine vigour, and natural value'. John Keats, Sir Walter Scott and Thomas Love Peacock are the key literary figures involved, although exactly why the changes occur 'remains something of a mystery' according to Knight.

The Romantics, especially Keats, and others in correspondence with him, turn Robin for the first time into 'a living, breathing, sensually realized identity with whom we can empathize' (2003, p. 103). For Keats the world of the greenwood is able to represent, again for the first time in the myth, a degree of criticism of the 'inorganic, alienated character of modern society' for a increasingly urbanized pre-Victorian England (2003, p. 105).

However, it is Sir Walter Scott who, in his 1819 novel *Ivanhoe*, relocates the narrative in the now familiar historical and national frame of the period of the so-called 'Norman Yoke'. The Norman Yoke of course is another myth; as we know from Chapter 2, the idea behind it is that the invading Normans of the eleventh century cruelly subjugated the Anglo-Saxon 'indigenous peoples' of the country. Scott revises the theory – initially utilized by eighteenth-century radicals supporting the French Revolution and the American War of Independence – that all (Norman) lords are oppressors; rather it is the race to which the lords belong that matters for Scott. So Locksley in the novel, who is clearly drawn as an Anglo-Saxon and therefore as an English Robin Hood without the name (until he is revealed as Robin Hood near the end – Knight explains the probable reason for changing the name on pp. 110–11 of his book), is a lord himself, but he is definitely *not* a Norman lord. Scott locates his story in the now familiar period of the 1190s when King Richard is away at the Crusades and the evil Prince John is running the country. This date of course invalidates the myth of the Norman–Saxon rivalry, since, as Knight points out (2003, p. 111), no Saxon lords remained by the 1190s, but this does not concern Scott and there is an insistence on the importance of race in the story from this point onwards.

Knight sums up this turn to the romantic, alongside other changes to the myth in early nineteenth-century novels, as making Robin Hood 'a gentleman who is in touch with the vitality of nature; he is not very active as a robber, has a lady and has youthful charm and patriotic energy' (2003, p. 118). And after discussing Peacock's novel, simply called *Robin Hood*, in which Maid Marian makes an important appearance and the greenwood becomes a 'source for true values and genuine law' (2003, p. 122), Knight describes the appearance of a romantic, heroic Robin who is 'decisively national, natural and masculine' (2003, p. 124). There are also touches of the slightly unknown nature of Robin's sexuality through this period – hints of an uncertainty in which both hetero- and homosexual features operate. This is 'Robin Hood Esquire', a mainly gentrified version of the myth. It is perhaps for our purposes one of the least interesting periods, except that we should note how much race and nationhood feature at this point as the Empire expands and nationalism waxes strongly.

The twentieth century

Knight points out immediately that the 'best comparison with the *Gest* is with the major films of the twentieth century' (2003, p. 152) – so we have 'Robin of Hollywood'. The rapid scene-shifting, focusing on one aspect of Robin's identity at a time, is reminiscent of the verse form of the early material. Here is a further reason for understanding the early material in such detail – for it is returned to us, albeit in a different genre, in modern versions of the myth.

Robin Hood's body remains important, particularly in this visual medium, and of course politically the story becomes internationalized while remaining true to the tradition – so that Robin even dies (again as in the *Gest*) in some of the films. What is remarkable through all the developments in films and cartoons is that 'the myth survives' (2003, p. 173).

In twentieth-century literature the myth seems to become even more malleable to the writer's own interests. It can be used as leftist propaganda (Geoffrey Trease, *Bows Against the Barons*, 1934) and there is a feminist take on the legend (Jennifer Roberson, *Lady of the Forest*, 1992) in which Maid Marian is at the forefront of the story.

Assessing the Robin Hood 'corpus'

Several methodologies are available to the reader who wants to understand what happens to the stories over the centuries (Knight 2003, pp. 202ff). A mythicist approach sees him variously as 'forest elf' or as some version of the Green Man legend or other so-called 'pagan' ideas. Yet these are not necessarily the popular understandings of the stories as experienced by millions of people. The question is, why is the myth so enduring when plenty of other similar figures have come and gone throughout the same period?

Knight points us suggestively to an anthropological solution to this conundrum. Following an article by Joseph Nagy (1999), his answer is that Robin Hood is ultimately a liminal figure, one who exists betwixt and between on almost every front. We noted this in the earlier material and review it again here.

We find Robin Hood portrayed first as a yeoman, located socially between gentry and commoners. In the greenwood, but negotiating the city/town life of the Sheriff. In the East Midlands of England, between north and south, at the gateway to the north across the Trent at Nottingham. Living in the eternal spring between winter and summer. Toing and froing between the authority of King and Sheriff, which both affirms and subverts their governance. A model Christian lay person, located between priest and ordinary laity. Later, one who stands between rich and poor, and later still, between men and women. Thus Nagy can conclude (1999, p. 425):

> The Robin Hood narrative tradition originated in medieval English society; but the values which these narratives communicated were relevant in the post-medieval world as well, and the liminal context in which they were expressed continued to exert a fascination. Thus, though some of this liminality (e.g. Robin as existing between yeomanry and the gentry) became outmoded with the changes that society underwent, the Robin Hood narratives remained popular down to the nineteenth century. They continued to function as myth, featuring a liminal world

that mirrors and interacts with the social world and characters whose adventures are an indirect expression of the values of the world from which they are seemingly alienated.

I believe such liminality plays itself out even in the very latest version of 'Robin of Hollywood', the 2010 film starring Russell Crowe. The film alternates between depicting with historical accuracy a twelfth-century England and France and completely reinventing the story in interesting but fantastical ways. It combines the pre-Reformation yeoman Robin Hood with the Norman Yoke legend and the development of Magna Carta. At the film's release there was huge controversy about Russell Crowe's accent; although having supposedly been coached to deliver his lines in an accent reminiscent of the medieval north of England, he seems unable to maintain any vocal consistency during the film. Many people think he sounds more Irish than English at points. Perhaps Crowe is caught betwixt and between even in voicing the hero. In the attempt to represent the reality of Robin Hood, the issue of Robin's fundamental liminality is played out once again.

In the anthropological study of rites of passage that Victor Turner's theory of liminality is based on, the limen (literally 'the edge') is located outside the African village. Secret and scary, it is nevertheless a place of transformation for children who become adults through the circumcision ceremonies that take place there. It is where change happens. Yet, importantly, it is not an end in itself but always points to the restoration of normal life and structure beyond the rite itself – when the adults return home. We have seen this principle operating time and time again in the Robin Hood stories. Authority is only questioned, threatened or even attacked in order that it might be restored – perhaps more justly – in the end, while the frailty of our rulers is understood. It is eternal spring only because we know autumn and winter will come in time. The rich are robbed and the poor benefit, not because this should be the permanent state of things but because we all recognize the basic inequalities and unfairness of life.

This thesis is confirmed by the evidence that we have accumulated about the boundaries of the myth. Robin Hood can become too gentrified, can be 'co-opted' by the great and the good, as in the work of Ben Jonson quoted above, but then he loses his energy and power. Neither however can he be so radical as to overthrow the system completely – the Luddites have to transcend the myth. Although a communist Robin is a possibility, does it really not destroy the story in some basic way?

In addition Knight shows how there are throughout the centuries 'increased periods of Robin Hood activity' (2003, p. 207) which seem to coincide with times when 'government has been overtly and consciously repressive'. These are of course times of transition and change in themselves – periods of liminality – and it is therefore no surprise that the myth is turned to as a 'safety valve' at such moments (2003, p. 209). Yet Robin Hood, because of the liminality of his persona and context, is never ultimately a revolutionary figure: 'The myth contains no plans for genuine redistribution, no new electoral system, no models of political organization that might actually work better.'

So 'In the heart of England lives a legend' – not in its head or its feet or hands, but in the heart. Our final task in this chapter is to summarize how the English characteristics identified by Kate Fox are found in the myths, thus making Robin Hood foundational to our culture.

Robin Hood – foundational to Englishness?

The first thing that hopefully has struck home in this chapter is the way in which Robin Hood holds the 'middle ground'. The liminal figure ultimately exists in between different extremes in order to re-establish the status quo. Thus *moderation* is characteristic of the stories as a whole. Robin Hood fits with the English notion of how politics should be: not revolutionary but holding to the elusive, if deeply ingrained notion of 'middle England'. Not far away is the *hypocrisy* in the stories that although wrongs are righted, nothing really changes in the overall scheme of things – which might lead to the *Eeyorishness* of believing that this is simply the way things normally are. There is also not a little of the violence and even hooliganism of English *social dis-ease* on display. A good fight isn't a bad thing, especially when you've been wronged – and it certainly beats having to sit down and negotiate face to face.

Fair play is strongly represented in the Robin Hood tradition, especially in the post-Reformation 'Norman Yoke' stories. Robin is restoring fairness in the face of 'bad' King John and the Sheriff of Nottingham. Taking from the rich and giving to the poor has to be the ultimate expression of establishing fairness. He and his small band of followers quickly become the underdogs whom we all cheer for against the might of the state – especially since they fight in general with *courtesy* and *modesty*. Inviting your victims to dine with you on the King's deer, as happens in the *Gest* stories, epitomizes this characteristic. Neither does Robin seek fame and fortune for his exploits. Whether he lives or dies, it seems he wants nothing more, having righted wrongs, than to settle down with Maid Marian.

We have discovered too how inevitably *class* drives the legends, as embodied both in Robin's membership of the emerging yeoman middle class before the Reformation and his status as the fallen lord after it. In the 2010 film *Robin Hood*, our hero starts as a yeoman and rises to the status of lord by having that status bestowed upon him – whether it 'fits' him or not is another matter! Perhaps there is a further aspect of hypocrisy lurking here in how class works in the stories. Robin's relation-ship with his followers also presents an opportunity for class relationships to be explored as the Merry Men come from different sections of society.

There is plenty of understated English *humour* in the stories, such as the deliberate irony – which, as we observed, we don't actually notice any more – in the name of Little John. The nature of Merry Men after all is to have fun together. Finally, there is something of English *empiricism* in the pragmatic way that Robin goes about his business while always returning to an earthy common-sense life in the forest.

There is no doubt that Englishness oozes out of the Robin Hood legends and we can be justifiably proud that the values encapsulated in the stories are now known worldwide.

... and in relation to the gospel?

I remarked earlier in the chapter how Robin's greenwood kingdom resonates with the *basilea* of the New Testament, not entirely but in several ways. Jesus, the lord of the kingdom, is one who has come down and is in-between; an outlaw who despite dealing with rich and poor, powerful and powerless still dies as an outlaw. He creates community (predominantly male community) around himself – a kind of *koinonia*. We could go on.

Yet there are discontinuities too. Robin's world is almost always a violent one, in which righteous violence is accepted as the norm, whereas Jesus' kingdom is a peaceable one where the need for sacrifice is overcome. There is seemingly no eschatological dimension to the greenwood; does it then offer real hope to change the world? These are some of the questions we will address in the next chapter as we bring the gospel and Englishness into dialogue together.

Perhaps what is most attractive about the Robin Hood myth, however, is that it provides a geographical location for the possibilities that the kingdom offers – something that remains elusive in the New Testament idea. There is a place in the heart of England where things don't have to be as they normally are.

5

English inculturation – face to face and eye to eye?

At the outset I want to emphasize that this chapter is only a beginning of the exploration of the integration of 'Christ and culture' in England today. In Chapter 1 we discovered how inculturation is a process and not an end-point and in Chapter 2 how England itself is a fluid idea. The main body of this chapter reports on the findings of the participants when the adult learning course associated with this book was run several times in different locations. But first let me remind you of how we got here and the purpose of this journey of discovery.

We explored in Chapter 1 the importance of the incarnation to the Christian faith – 'the Word became flesh and made his dwelling among us' (John 1.14, NIV). The Church therefore forgets to engage with culture at its absolute peril. Perhaps the rise of groups like the English Defence League is partly due to the Church's lack of engagement with cultural questions in this period after Christendom. The relationship between faith and culture is a two-way street characterized by Walls' indigenizing and pilgrim principles. Faith is not so much about assenting to some core irreducible truths; rather it embodies and lives those truths within a culture. Culture is therefore holy ground, and to be taken seriously as a source of revelation. We can expect to find ways in which the gospel both resonates with and challenges English culture. As we do that we will discover how the English, and particularly the English Christian, can become more human and more free – we want to further humanity among the English.

So we now move from the description of English culture to some measure of prescription about it. A proper evaluation needs to take place and the initial results from the course presented in this chapter will help us to do that. One of the advantages of the way the course is run is that most of the material generated is recorded on flip-chart pads and can be kept, written up and reflected upon later. The course has been run by me, the author, and in order to prove that it wasn't solely dependent on me it has also been run by someone else using only the explanatory manual for the facilitator. I am very grateful to all the participants who took part in the pilot programmes and who generated the material presented in this chapter. While I believe sufficient 'data' has been generated by these initial courses to present a full picture (they were run in both urban and rural contexts), I hope that the course will be delivered many more times in the future; that is why this is simply a beginning of English inculturation work.

I shall first present the course participants' findings, derived from their imaginative theological 'play' both in the English metaphorical worlds created by the six sayings and in the worlds from the Bible or the tradition that were placed alongside them during each session. Other useful data are the insights generated along the way and the final position statements of the group members, which were all recorded.[1] I shall then spend some time reflecting on the results and the themes which emerge from each session and ask some relevant questions for you, the reader, to reflect upon, should you wish. I hope also that if you are planning to run the course yourself, this chapter will be excellent material to interact with either before or after you begin.

Finally, at the end of the chapter, I shall draw some initial conclusions and a summary of the English inculturation project from the data presented.

---

[1] All material generated in the groups is presented here in anonymous form. We did not record the proposed actions of the participants at the end of the studies, partly to keep these too both personal and anonymous.

Moderation: 'Don't rock the boat'

In the pilot groups there was initially a fairly strong negative reaction to entering this world. The saying implies that we are in the boat together, while the boat offers a significant and obvious boundary to the outside. It felt boring, stagnant, calm and possibly suppressed or repressed, with little space for an individual to stand out. However, once the question of transforming the metaphorical world was addressed, the mood changed and interesting themes emerged. If the boat had a specific destination, rather than simply floating aimlessly across the water, then it was felt that the community in the boat could really pull together. It would work towards the collective purpose, perhaps even laying aside individual needs and developing on the journey a democratic system of decision making, teamwork and shared values. On arrival at the destination there could be a real celebration of what had been achieved, a celebration to which specific learning, fellowship and 'oneness' could all contribute.

A diverse range of biblical references was placed alongside the metaphor in the different groups; some of these references, such as the suggested passage of Jesus being asked to leave the Gerasenes after healing the demoniac in Mark 5 and Jesus throwing the money changers out of the temple, were in direct contrast to it. There were suggestions of communitarian passages such as 1 Corinthians 12 and Pilate washing his hands of Jesus, although these were not eventually taken up. A further very interesting reflection took place in relation to the verse 'be still and know that I am God', which placed stillness and silence alongside moderation.

Participants in the groups developed several helpful insights from their reflections – not least noting again the importance of the boundary that the boat offers, which raised questions of how an individual might get out of or into it, since that of itself would imply some rocking. There appeared to be a certain lack of individual 'freedom' on the non-rocking boat.

Positions identified by the participants at the end of the study showed a fundamental tension within the English reflex of moderation; this was summed up by the person who quoted the comedian Billy Connolly, who apparently said 'Everything in moderation, including moderation!' Several members of the groups recognized the importance of rocking the boat – but in a way that might be assertive or productive of significant change rather than aggressive or destructive. Some members were happy to own their moderation and leave it to others to be their leaders and risk-takers. The question of discernment therefore arose; knowing when is the right time to do some rocking and how to go about it in the best way. Again this contrasted stillness and silence with moderation.

Several themes and further questions arise from the pilot groups' data.

The boundary of the community and its destination

The proverbial saying 'don't rock the boat' raises for us the question of whether the English feel as if they are essentially beleaguered and thrown together in a boat surrounded constantly by a dangerous sea. Is this another aspect of the island mentality which sets 'us against the world', or at least against the 'other' – those without the boat?[2] However, the reaction of Christians to the saying was encouraging, given this starting point. Perhaps, in these days, to be a Christian is to have 'rocked the boat' already; or it might be better to say that Christians have had their boat rocked and so tension is exhibited in them between recognizing the pull to moderation and wanting to do some rocking. The idea of a boat is of course related in the Bible and theology, first to the ark in Genesis and then to the ark of salvation, the Church. Thus the positive side of the ramifications of this saying is the potential of what can happen in the boat, especially if it has a specific destination. Needless to say, Christians do have a destination and purpose and live in the light of the

---

[2] Kate Fox (2004, p. 407) thinks that geography may well play a part in determining English characteristics, especially as there are some similarities between the English and the Japanese, who both live on small overcrowded islands. However, ultimately she suggests there is no simple answer as to why the English are the way they are – that is just how they are.

coming future kingdom. We know, though, that a critique of this 'ark of salvation' model of church is that it can become closed to the outside world and stuck in certain patterns of behaviour. All of which raises the next question.

How does change happen?

Kate Fox reckons (2004, p. 403) that only 14 per cent of us are risk seekers and we will have to rely on these people to bring about change. I am not so sure. The evidence from our pilot reflections shows that significant work can still be done on reaching a destination without rocking the boat too much along the way, but this requires a degree of interaction and mutual self-giving which is unusual in human society. Perhaps moderation has served us better as a nation than we might think. I don't believe in any case that moderation necessarily precludes change. It does mean it will be slower and there will be more 'checks and balances' on the way, but is that a bad thing? What do you think? There was no equivalent to the French Revolution in England, but are we better or worse off for that?

Stillness and moderation

Finally we address this theme, another which emerged in the pilot studies. Might a corporate silence, stillness – a waiting on God – give us the clue as to how English moderation can truly be redeemed? Finding the still point is the ultimate in not 'rocking the boat', but in a strange way it is not moderate but rather extreme. I think the participants who worked on this idea were suggesting that holding stillness and silence before God is a way to decide whether to rock the boat or not.

Humorous moaning: 'Typical!'

Inevitably there was a lot of laughter during the reflection upon this subject. On entering the 'Typical!' world, it became clear that it is a necessary place that helps us to cope – a survival mechanism for 'getting through' whatever comes our way. It can lead to a sense of defeatism and depressing self-fulfilling sarcasm, as we get stuck in the stories we tell about ourselves. We expect the worst and then it happens! But that is not the only direction it can go in. Perhaps we can be so 'drowned' in the experience – letting ourselves become subjects of it – that we eventually come out the other side; that very subjectivity seems to offer us some helpful objectivity in its turn. Laughter in itself takes us out of the immediate difficulty; there is a solidarity in the mutual moaning and a recognition underneath that things are probably not as bad as everyone thinks.

The 'Typical!' world is also a place where it becomes possible to find acceptance, particularly of faults and failure. In one of the groups it became clear that, at its best, humorous moaning can be a preparation for getting beyond the immediate situation and discovering newness and even joy within it. The example was given of getting caught in a heavy rain shower and becoming so wet that there is no going back, so then every puddle can be splashed in and what was miserable becomes real fun. As someone put it in an insight, 'Getting beyond being immersed in the chaos and beginning to dance with it!'

In this study each of the groups happened to use the same biblical text to lay alongside the saying. It was a contrasting text: John 5.8, the healing of the paralysed man who has been 'waiting' for his healing at the pool of Siloam for a very long time. It follows immediately as Jesus' response to the 'Typical!' reaction in verse 7, where the man explains how he is never able to get into the healing waters in time. Here a surprising, challenging and risk-taking word is offered, and it proves to be transforming. It picks up immediately where the moaning left off. Thus, as someone said in their position statement, the gospel is positively subversive in going beyond the 'Typical!'. Nevertheless the 'Typical!' reaction can be a kind of preparation for the gospel to take hold. Again the group data offers us several themes to reflect upon.

Laughter and faith

It is perhaps fair to say that there is not enough laughter in the Church, and here our English culture has something to teach Christians. As Fox points out, there is a clear taboo on 'earnestness' embedded in the English psyche, along with 'a stubborn refusal to be duped or taken in by fine rhetoric, and a mischievous delight in pricking balloons of pomposity and self-importance' (2004, p. 403). We are prone to take ourselves very seriously in the Church, and when dealing with some issues of faith this is probably right and proper. However, we have also noted how the gospel is able to subvert and turn upside-down the normalities of life – which is not a million miles from the task of the stand-up comic. When talking of revolutions, Fox thinks that we English simply have satire instead of uprisings and attempts to overturn the status quo.

A radical acceptance and solidarity?

What seems to be happening in the average kind of English humour is a way of accepting not only the small ordinary disasters of life but also some of the bigger things – we could think in this context of 'gallows humour'. Being realistic about our situation, being able to see it for what it is and make some ironic, mocking or sarcastic remark about it, takes away some of its power over us and sets us on an equal footing with each other. Is this not a place the Christian would want to bless? Acknowledging our weaknesses and failures is part and parcel of everyday discipleship, and so much the better if we can admit them to each other via humour. As we have seen, this humorous wallowing in our difficult experiences could just be a partner to fatalism or giving up in defeat, but it can also be a step on to something better. What do you think? Is English humour simply a release mechanism or does it have the potential to fulfil a greater purpose?

A preparation for newness

Given the data from the pilot reflections, I think English humour does have the potential at least to take us to a place of readiness and openness for a transforming word or action. This place, as we have seen, is one of objectivity borne of deep subjectivity –

almost as if through wallowing in the dirt we are able to rise from it. The dance emerges from the chaos. It could be that here, hidden away in English culture, is what some missiologists have called the *praeparatio evangelica*, the preparation for the gospel. This is the idea that all cultures have some elements which are precursors to hearing and accepting the good news of God – small foundations upon which the whole edifice of faith can be built. It is a similar idea to that we discussed in Chapter 1, the idea of the translatability of the gospel, and here is one place where it is translatable into English culture. We will return to this idea in our final chapter when we look at the implications of the study of Englishness for doing mission in England.

Privacy: 'An Englishman's home is his castle'

The metaphor of home as castle was a deeply suggestive and fruitful one for all the pilot groups and perhaps one of the easiest to enter into. An immediate and apparent paradox arose within it, one which exposed and unmasked the saying as a myth. While a castle can be a safe and secure haven, it is also highly visible from miles around. It can offer feasts and celebrations in some parts, but there are also usually dungeons somewhere else. While the drawbridge is down it is open to the world, but pull it up because there are attackers in the offing and the castle turns into one big prison.

In one of the groups it was pointed out that, as we have already seen, the saying was popularized by Charles Dickens in *Great Expectations*. Mr Pip is shown around Wemmick's 'castle', which, despite being a tiny cottage, boasts a gun turret that is fired every evening at nine o'clock and a kitchen garden that would 'hold out a devil of a time' in case of siege. Perhaps what's more important is the boundary the castle provides for Wemmick himself: 'the office is one thing, and private life another. When I go into the office, I leave the Castle behind me, and when I come into the Castle I leave the office behind me.'

Thus the redeeming of the castle occurs, the participants found, when these boundaries are held more lightly, when the outsider is allowed in, when hospitality is offered, when – as one group noted – more windows are put in and the whole becomes less defensive.

The biblical reflections covered a number of different passages this time, from the suggested entry of Jesus into the locked upper room in John 20 and the challenge to 'build houses and live in them' from Jeremiah 29 (REB) to the promise of many mansions 'in my father's house' in John 14. In relating these to the privacy metaphor, several helpful lines of discussion emerged. First of all was the importance of home for the human being – the sense that home is a place not simply to exist in but one in which to share the deepest and most intimate relationships with others and with God. There was also the sense that while such a home may be yet to be, in our earthly homes we can at least aim at holding elements of the heavenly one. Safety and security at home are important – a couple of people were struck during the study with how difficult it is to live without a happy home, or even as a refugee, and another with how much our homes are tied up with our identity and 'how they tell stories about us'. Nevertheless the reflections consistently showed the importance to Christians of the giftedness, inclusiveness and openness of home. In fact it would be difficult to achieve this openness without the security and identity afforded by home, and perhaps the key to achieving it was overcoming the fear that created the need for the thick boundary of the castle in the first place. No, the boundary does not need to be fully removed, but it seemed important that Jesus was able to come and go at will through the walls of the upper room and brought peace and the absence of fear with him. In contrast to the cold, dark and draughty castle, Jesus brought light and warmth into the room as he lit up the faces of those present. Thus, if the Lord is the 'head' of the household, the castle has the potential to be a true home.

What about the meaning of your home? How much is it a gift and how strongly are its boundaries held – and why? (For example, how high are your fences/hedges? Does your home provide a buffer between work and domestic life, as for Wemmick?) How could it become more open and inclusive?

It is difficult not to get the feeling that this particular study strikes at the heart of Englishness, given that privacy is related in Fox's thought to the core English characteristic of 'social dis-ease' – our chronic difficulty in relating to others. What was interesting was that in the groups people in their insights got in touch with other core elements of Englishness. Thus we had a vision of everyone joining in St George's Day celebrations, while someone else quoted Shakespeare's eloquent lines on England and its meaning from *King Richard II* (Act 2, Scene 1):

> This royal throne of kings, this sceptred isle,
> This earth of majesty, this seat of Mars,
> This other Eden, demi-paradise,
> This fortress built by Nature for herself
> Against infection and the hand of war,
> This happy breed of men, this little world,
> This precious stone set in the silver sea,
> Which serves it in the office of a wall
> Or as a moat defensive to a house,
> Against the envy of less happier lands –
> This blessed plot, this earth, this realm, this England.

A connection is made here by Shakespeare between the English nation and a house. We touched on the effect of geography on English self-understanding in the first reflection in this chapter and here the question is raised again. This time, though, there is a mythological, even spiritual element to the question. England is sceptred, another Eden, a blessed plot, while also being a natural fortress where the sea acts as a defensive moat to the 'house', which is the nation. If this is the case and Shakespeare's understanding of Englishness has filtered through into the nation's consciousness, then we can understand our house, our home, in these same 'holy' terms as sceptred, precious, blessed. Just as we came to understand the whole field of culture to be a domain of the holy, we have now discovered the holiness of the English home. Here is another domain that can point our people towards God and a relationship with the One who is ultimately relational.

Fair play: 'Well, to be fair . . .'

The saying used in this study changed during the course of the piloting programme, showing at the very least that action was taken from the review after each run through of the course. Originally we were working with 'Fair's fair', but this was felt to be slightly too closed a saying and not so well related to the English value of fair play as 'Well, to be fair . . .' This latter saying usually precedes some sentence which equalizes a previous statement, which sees the other side of things. However, I think we can still safely use here the data collected from all the studies.

A world characterized by fair play, as seen by the participants in the course, is one of equality of opportunity and freedom of speech, but possibly one which stifles difference and is a bit boring, dull and mediocre (in this sense it seems related to the 'don't rock the boat' world). Nevertheless it is a place where the weak can be supported and the underdog considered important. It is a place of tolerance, where others are respected and acknowledged. At its best this world can be a place where everyone can better themselves while being content with what they have. Its inhabitants can finally come to realize their true potential, while also appreciating and wanting the best for what others can achieve.

For the biblical reflection the groups either used the parable of the Prodigal Son from Luke 15 (the elder brother's outburst, 'What have you ever given me?') or the parable of the Workers in the Vineyard from Matthew 20, where those who have worked an hour are paid the same as those who worked all day ('We worked in the hot sun all day long!' – v. 12, CEV). One of the groups worked hard on how the elder brother's world could be transformed, especially since he seemed to encapsulate something of the hard-working, faithful, reliable and uncomplaining Englishman, keeping a stiff upper lip until everything broke out. Some felt that one lesson to be learned here was not to let resentment build up via the stiff upper lip but to 'talk, talk, talk!'. Others realized in their position statements that to have fairness as a value 'oils social intercourse' but also has its limits.

Supporting the underdog, caring for the marginalized, tolerance

It is not a big step for the English, given the value they place on fair play and giving the underdog a chance, to move from that to caring for the marginalized and the outsider. In fact we noted David Blunkett's remarks on this very theme in Chapter 2. The Bible constantly seems to turn upside-down the value placed by the ancient world on the elder son; from the blessing offered to Abel and not Cain, through Jacob overcoming Esau and King David rising to the heights, to the younger son in Jesus' parable. Kate Fox thinks that the value of fair play is often mistaken for 'both socialism and conservatism, and even Christianity' (2004, p. 407), as so much of English morality is about fair play. But there may be a real congruence here between English fair play and biblical values which support the younger, the weaker, the marginalized. What do you think? Do you notice this kind of connection in yourself or in others?

The groups mentioned tolerance in the studies more than once. So there may also be another connection to be made from the notion of fair play to the evidence of how we behave towards outsiders, one showing that, despite a surface racism in some people and places in England, in general we are pragmatically tolerant of the outsider. How else could a version of an exotic dish from the East have become our favourite food? Once again we have the foundation material to work on in one part of our culture for combating the more unhelpful traits in other parts.

English egalitarianism

Nevertheless there are two sides to the concept of fair play in English culture – in an insight, one of the participants called them 'caring and critical'. On the one hand, as we have seen above, there is something good and true about allowing everyone a fair chance. It doesn't mean we don't recognize that there are winners and losers among us, just that we believe everyone should have an equal go. As someone pointed out in another insight, there is nothing more unequal than treating everyone equally, since not everyone has exactly the same starting point.

Kate Fox believes that there is a polite English egalitarianism (2004, p. 407) which is not just critical but hypocritical since it is concerned with the appearance of fairness – concealing and hiding embarrassing inequalities and differences. She gives the example of the convoluted transaction by way of which a customer obliquely offers an English bartender a tip by asking whether he or she would like a drink ('And one for yourself?'), thus emphasizing the bartender's equality with the customer over his or her service role (pp. 95ff). This is a problem for us (and, as I have just realized while writing this, for me!). Not everyone is the same, we all have different gifts and abilities, and trying to gloss over these differences is unhelpful in the long term. It is counter-cultural for us to recognize overtly and openly the differences between us. In contrast, the kingdom that Jesus inaugurates in the Gospels faces up to the vast differences in first-century Palestinian society and is prepared to do something about them. It seems we are probably ready for the next study now.

Class: I know my place

Participants in this study were not reluctant to discuss the theme of class. Indeed it seemed that many welcomed with relief the opportunity to talk about something that touches all of our lives each day while remaining almost completely hidden. The sketch from which the saying 'I know my place' was taken is an extremely helpful starting point, not least because of the looking up and down the social scale that goes on. In one group this behaviour was seriously and profoundly challenged when members realized the world of the saying might be redeemed by not looking up or down at others but rather eye to eye or face to face. Such an action would require letting go of resentment and superiority or inferiority, members thought.

Of course this can only be done if we are each happy in our own skin, our own class. As someone said very simply in their position statement, 'I am middle class.' Another was clear that those who are closer to the class boundaries or who have moved recently across them are less secure in their class identity. The course suggests that, in this particular study, a relevant reflection from the Christian tradition rather than the Bible might be a story from the life of William Carey, the Baptist missionary to India, a man who was very happy to own and live in the place and the class he had started from.[3] On the other hand, one of the groups tested the saying to destruction by imagining what would happen if class were genetically determined so that everyone had to accept it!

However, the results of laying the story of William Carey alongside the saying were perhaps not as helpful as when the saying of Jesus, 'The first shall be last and the last first', was used as the starting point for the comparative reflection. What was interesting here, as this world was entered into and played with, was the realization that it eventually makes everyone come first if they are prepared to take the last place. This is not dissimilar to the insight of the biblical story-teller Trevor Dennis, who believes that in the parable of the Prodigal Son, the father actually ends up with *two* elder sons rather than just one.[4] The younger son cannot be reinstated to his former position, since he forfeited it, but is offered an entirely new position created by the father and on a par with his brother. Thus – another key insight – we can understand class differences in a circular fashion rather than a purely hierarchical one. I learnt the phrase 'clogs to clogs (in three generations)', which refers to the energy required to escape from poverty – symbolized by the archetypal working-class footwear – in the first place, but that same energy

---

[3] The story of William Carey can be found in Week 5 of the Englishness course. See Appendix, p. 148.

[4] As recounted in a talk in Southwell Minster on 8 May 2010.

not being present in the next, gentrified generation and thus the return to the status of clog-wearers by the third one. Finally, others realized that if the last grab first place by force there is a problem, but if there is consent by the first to live as the last then we are imitating Christ. We can reflect further on this theme below.

So where does all this leave you, the reader? What would it be like to look in a full-length mirror and name your class to yourself through what you see? Is it possible to note the hundreds of times a day we make instant judgments about others because of their clothes, speech and behaviour? Can we rise above these to look these others in the eye, rather than their handbag or at the cut of their trousers?

Christ the classless one?

I am nevertheless left with the sense, as an Englishman writing this, that all such talk of class is slightly tacky if not downright dirty. In the groups there was, alongside the realization that we should own our own class, a feeling that Christians should be also somehow classless and transcend class boundaries, perhaps because their identity is now found elsewhere. Thus, going further, if we could understand Christ as classless we would be able to see Christ in everyone, as someone's position stated.

I wonder whether this is one of the drivers of depictions of Christ in England in the last 150 or so years, since appearance is such a deep and strong signifier of class for us. Christ is usually dressed in some nondescript white robe that would not be out of place doubling as a nightdress. Yes, in Holman Hunt's *Light of the World* there are hints of kingship in the cloak and the crown, but that is all. More typical are the hugely popular prints of Harold Copping from the early twentieth century (an internet search will quickly offer lots of his work) or Margaret Tarrant (look up *The Lesser Brethren*) from a little later. Even Brian of Monty Python fame, despite *not* being Jesus, is no more imaginatively dressed.

It probably isn't helpful to read back English class categories into the Gospel accounts of Jesus' origins in the 'carpenter's' workshop,[5] while other cultures are able to offer pictures of Jesus as he may appear in their own particularity (as is suggested through the CMS/USPG *Christ We Share* material in the accompanying course). Yet, although he is white and has a beard, Jesus as depicted in England couldn't look less English. This is the reason why the course challenges people to come up with ideas for 'showing off' an 'English Christ' to the world. But it proved not to be that easy, perhaps partly because of what we have referred to as our 'polite egalitarianism' – our embarrassment at this class talk.

Some serious implications for mission in England are identified here. I think it is fair to say that churches divided clearly along class lines in the Industrial Revolution and beyond, and probably have never recovered. Again we shall return to this issue in the next chapter.

Courtesy: 'Sorry!'

In a repeat of their experience in week one, participants found it uncomfortable to enter the world of saying 'sorry' in our peculiarly English way. It feels irritating, evasive, falsely self-deprecating, manipulative and somewhat ridiculous when we face up to it. Someone described it as 'puppy behaviour'. There are good reasons for it – it can be self-protective and defuses conflict and allows for our own imperfections. It can be a safe, pleasant and contented place. Not many would argue against the importance of displaying courtesy in our behaviour, yet the way we go about it may preclude a more open and honest relationship. If we are going to get beyond the surface cheap apology, we need to let go of false humility and develop a deeper sense of self-awareness, a process that will lead us to assertiveness and freedom.

Someone raised the question in an insight as to whether we English Christians can be too courteous and polite with God. And then there is the question of whether our constant 'sorrying' devalues the currency, as we might say, as it doesn't seem

---

[5] By all accounts, the word used for Joseph's trade is better translated as referring to the building trade in general rather than the specific skill of carpentry.

to cost us very much. So it was helpful in the biblical reflections that the groups chose some rather deeper apologies to work with – Job saying to God his creator and seeming tormentor, 'I talked about things I did not understand' (Job 42.3, my translation) and Zacchaeus in Luke 19 repaying four times over what he has defrauded. These took the groups to places of silent communion and, interestingly, again to seeing face to face with our own eyes; also to a place where through repentance a corner is turned and, as Desmond Tutu has said, a new possible future which is open and honest emerges through forgiveness.

In the position statements, there was a recognition of the shallowness of the English 'sorry' – that it doesn't seem to go far enough or deep enough. We need to reflect more honestly on what drives us to be so apologetic for ourselves. What do you think? Do you find yourself apologizing needlessly for your presence, intrusion, interruption? Again the theme of security in our identity and our self-awareness arises. Nevertheless, there is something good that we want to affirm about courtesy which is not arrogant or macho, and given that we are used to saying sorry, perhaps it isn't a very big step to go deeper with the idea.

Overall what is interesting to note is how this study has repeated themes which emerged in the other studies – the importance of silence and a meditative approach to God; assertiveness and security of identity; seeing face to face and eye to eye.

Summary and conclusions

Let me start this final section by stating the obvious, but nevertheless important fact that all the participants proved themselves to be English! What I mean is that they recognized themselves in the six sayings and metaphors and there was no sense that they were not able to enter into the worlds created by them. In addition to this, as Christians they were also able to do the inculturation work of looking for the indigenizing and pilgrim elements in their own English culture through the methodology of the course. We discovered how a lot of Englishness is a survival mechanism, a way of getting through, and in that sense, since the English are still here, we can see that it works! Even that point is worth making; as any development worker will tell you, what you don't do when trying to improve indigenous agricultural methods is stop overnight what the people have been doing for centuries – for at the very least it has got them to this point. Let's accept and own our Englishness.

When we did begin to accept it, a sense of mutuality and solidarity that wasn't exclusive in any way began to emerge around the participants' joint identity. This is why I believe people who are not originally English but have been living here long enough to have some awareness of English characteristics will be able to participate fully in the course and make a real contribution to it. Participants recognized that the strengthening of cultural identity through interacting with our own culture on the course actually allows us to be more open to the 'other' – something I have observed in several different contexts, both here and in Africa. This in itself is the beginning of 'furthering humanity' among us, and perhaps the beginning of a thought we will pursue in the next chapter – that, for Christians in this country, a common exploration of Englishness would be a way into mission with their compatriots.

Throughout the courses I facilitated there was evidence that members became increasingly conscientized and aware of their innate Englishness as the weeks went on. They noticed things in the media that sparked with them in a new way, or they brought in artefacts, stories or poems that related to the themes being discussed. From time to time it was difficult to own our own culture and that uncomfortable feeling I have felt occasionally in writing this book came over the group. All in all though, while being conscientized about our culture is a constant challenge, it clearly had begun to make a difference for most of the members.

What then have we begun to learn about the relationship between English culture, as we have defined it through these proverbs and sayings, and the gospel?

I believe that any of the places we explored via the sayings could, with some nurturing and encouragement, be taken as a starting point for something good and true to emerge – the indigenizing principle. In some places we could see how a particular theme could be taken in the opposite direction – for instance, the boundaried nature of the island and our homes might be a recipe for excluding the outsider, but it need not be.

The fact that we were on holy ground most of the time was evidenced by the occasions when the reflections took the members to stillness and silence, emphasizing the importance of meditating upon a particular aspect of culture so that we might properly discern in which direction to take it towards the God who was ultimately behind it. This was true, for example, of fair play, which can lead to tolerance and the destruction of bigotry. There is no clear distinction here between the indigenizing and the pilgrim principles, reinforcing what we learnt in Chapter 1 – that inculturation is indeed a dynamic process.

Humour too, we discovered, was much more of an ally to the gospel than we have given it credit for in the Church. In a sense that was a challenge from the culture to the faith rather than the other way round, which shows that we had been in genuine dialogue. The holy nature of the English home, when put at the disposal of one who had no home and when not restricted by the thickness of its walls, was another place of real possibility and newness.

Where then was the challenge from the gospel to the culture – the pilgrim principle? We have already noted the importance of becoming secure in our identity and the help that offers us when addressing our tendency to insularity and exclusiveness. In addition it was interesting how the need for assertiveness rather than aggression came up in the course data more than once. That is the idea that often we over-compensate for our insecurity and inability to relate by becoming aggressive. This is related in my mind to the suggestive idea that arose during the discussion on class for developing face-to-face or eye-to-eye relationships in order to overcome the divisiveness of 'us and them' attitudes, both up and down the social scale. If Kate Fox is right, and at the heart of Englishness is a 'dis-ease' when it comes to our social relationships, it would seem sensible to ask if that disease might be healed through seeing both God and each other 'face to face and eye to eye'.

Is it possible that Englishness provides a 'veil' for our faces which obscures not only our relationship with God but also our relationships with each other? If so we need to hear the words of St Paul to the Corinthians: 'whenever anyone turns to the Lord, the veil is taken away . . . where the Spirit of the Lord is, there is freedom. And we, who with unveiled faces all reflect the Lord's glory, are being transformed into his likeness with ever-increasing glory' (2 Cor. 3.16–18, NIV).

Unveiled faces and a secure identity, allied with godly freedom, would surely also help us with the problems we have identified with our polite egalitarianism, which so often ends up in hypocrisy and hiding the truth (back to veils again!).

Here then is a beginning, as I stated at the start of the chapter, of describing the inculturation project for the English. It is by no means exhaustive, but I hope it has given a real flavour of what is possible and excited you to go further with the project. All that remains in the final chapter is draw the threads of our work together and see what implications there might be deriving from this, perhaps novel approach, for the mission of God in our 'blessed plot'.

6

Mission in England as if culture matters

━━━━◆•◆•◆━━━━

As I hinted in the Introduction, Christendom is over, even if it isn't quite dead yet – or as someone put it to me recently, we are in its 'twilight'. There have been almost as many books proclaiming this fact published in the last ten years as there have been on Englishness. The two subjects are related, in the sense that once the centrality of the Church in the nation state (not just in England) is removed, the assumptions that have been made about culture and national religion under the aegis of Christendom can be pulled apart and re-examined.

Two of the best chroniclers of the current dilemma of the Church and what is to be done about it from within the Christian faith are John Drane (2000, 2005, 2008) and George Lings.[1] Drane describes himself these days as a 'spiritual consultant' to traditional and emerging churches rather than any kind of ordained minister, which neatly sums up his critique of where Christendom has got to. He believes that, in its current state, the Church in general offers an unattractive religiosity without much true spirituality at its heart. Lings works for the Church Army, which is currently transforming itself for the new era, and he offers a helpful picture in which the Christendom church lies at the bottom of a cultural valley, relying on the fact that the culture will naturally 'roll' people into it. Post Christendom the Church is located on the top of a steep cultural hill which rolls people away from church. It is important to note here that

---

[1] Lings' work is published in many short monographs called *Encounters on the Edge* and available from <http://www.encountersontheedge.org.uk/>.

Lings is using the word 'culture', I believe, a little differently from how we have been working with it in this study. It is much more the sociological 'plausibility structure' for the existence of the Christian faith that he is referring to. Our anthropological or semiotic definition goes somewhat deeper.

Thus sociologists and religious studies academics, particularly those outside faith, are generally very sceptical about the future of the Church. A full treatment of the movement away from religion and towards spirituality from the religious studies tradition is found in Paul Heelas and Linda Woodhead's *The Spiritual Revolution: Why Religion Is Giving Way to Spirituality* (2005). Some of the book presents empirical field research in the north of England which details the phenomenon on the ground. Callum Brown (2001), a sociologist, traces the demise of the Church over recent decades and concludes that there is only 'death' ahead. Grace Davie is more sympathetic, while noting the recent change to 'believing without belonging' (1994), although it could be argued, looking at the whole sweep of the history of 'Christian' England, that that is simply a return to a more normal state of affairs. It is also worth noting in Davie's work (2002) that Europe's lack of interest in religion is exceptional in worldwide terms, where if anything there is a burgeoning turn to the major faiths.

Another more recent book which brings the theme of this work together with the demise of the traditional Church is Cole Moreton's *Is God Still an Englishman? How We Lost Our Faith (But Found New Soul)* (2010). Moreton, a journalist, writes a semi-autobiographical account of the changes in attitudes to English religion since the early 1980s. Along the way he finds and then loses his own evangelical/charismatic Anglican faith, and he finishes the book enigmatically, making a pile of stones on a beach to symbolize the end of something while praying silently to whatever God might be for him now. It is quite difficult to separate the personal journey from the objective journalism in Moreton's writing, but he is surely right in declaring George Bernard Shaw's assertion that 'the ordinary Britisher imagines that God is an Englishman' to be untenable in the majority of

England in 2010 (his main arguments are summarized on pp. 283–5 of his book).

Isn't this a good thing though? To identify the whole of God with one nationality is at best heresy and at worst idolatry. On the other hand, we have seen how at the heart of Christianity is the incarnation of the *Logos* – the eternal Word dwelling or tabernacling in flesh at a particular time and place. The task for English Christians, therefore, if we are not to give up our faith altogether, is to bury the English God but to rediscover the English Christ. The purpose of this chapter is to offer some pointers as to how we might do this.

A word of caution before we get going. What is presented here is *not* the answer to the problems English churches face after a decade of this new millennium. There is no 'silver bullet' which will solve all our problems; Moreton documents how a few of these completely missed their targets (or never left the gun!) over the last 30 years, including the Decade of Evangelism, the March for Jesus and the Nine O'Clock Service (NOS). No, according to the sociologist of organizations, Ron Heifetz, we face the challenge of *adaptive change*.[2] That is, there are no technical changes we can make which will solve our problems; rather, we are consciously incompetent about what to do and can only experiment (or we could say 'play') to see what works – and we might expect experimental failures like NOS. All of which is a deeply spiritual task, as it requires us to stay with uncertainty, weakness and struggle while living by faith.

So, as the tide of Christendom goes out, can we recover a sense of mission in this country in ways that take culture seriously? My own reflection on the Decade of Evangelism was from the perspective of missing most of it, since I was working in Tanzania. However, on my return, what was clear to me was that mission as whole, while it was roundly condemned as a

---

[2] My friend Pat Keifert, a systematic theologian from the USA, gives as an extreme example of an adaptive challenge the need for the airline industry to find an alternative to fossil fuels as a means of propelling aeroplanes.

failure, was now on the agenda of all the churches across all theological traditions in a new and fresh way. This was in stark contrast to the position ten years earlier.

My own interest in missiology (much to my children's be-musement about the meaning of the word) was kindled about this time and I began to realize that a lot of the lessons learnt in doing mission across the world in the last two hundred years were now highly relevant in England itself (Rooms, 2005) – a situation which has also informed the trans-formation of the Anglican Church Mission Society in recent years from a mission agency to a missional order. Thus the research into and application of inculturation to the English context is my small contribution to this re-engagement with mission in our land.

I think the first step in engaging missionally with culture is to decide on one's contextual theology. Or, to put it in terms that we looked at in Chapter 1, where do we position ourselves on the faith–culture continuum which Stephen Bevans (2002) offers us? How far do we want to allow the greater authority to Scripture/tradition/'truth' at one end and culture/human creativity/context at the other? As you may have guessed by now, I lean towards the cultural end of the spectrum, not least because of my understanding, in missiological terms, of what is known as the *Missio Dei*.[3] This is the theological idea that God, by God's very nature, is missionary in creating and redeeming the world. Mission is the crossing of boundaries, and God crosses the boundary of Godself in making the universe and then entering the world in the flesh of Jesus Christ. Nothing then in this world is outside of God; while of course we cannot identify the material of the world with God, nevertheless it remains created and sustained by God. Thus, as we have already asserted, 'we can never be sure where God, or Christ, is not.'

---

[3] For an empirical study in the contemporary UK and Ireland of the receptivity of the *Missio Dei* in contrast to other approaches to mission, see Anne Richards, Nigel Rooms et al., *Foundations for Mission: A Study of Language, Theology and Praxis from the UK and Ireland Perspective* (London: CTBI, 2010).

The same is true of human culture, and it is the task of Christians to discern God within their culture at every point.

That has also been the task of this book, and the results of the data collected from the groups studying Englishness theologically show that we can be mostly, but not universally, positive about English culture at its deeper levels. We can agree with Shakespeare that England is a chosen, blessed and sceptred place as a starting point to venturing out of the Church on to that steep hill inhabited by people who find it difficult to believe the Church has much to offer. We can set out knowing that there will be places we can discover Christ afresh.

And when we step out of the Church these days, we need to recognize that out there is a multi-religious world in which we have to find our own place and space and where we are obliged to earn the right to be heard. For instance, Moreton (2010) has a whole chapter on the resurgence of paganism among the English, which he believes is part of our search for new 'soul' (he never actually defines soul, but it is an interesting aim). So we set out as Christians in what the missiologist David Bosch called 'bold humility' to find ways to meet with people like pagans and share our understanding of faith in Christ. We cannot, and indeed should not, return to the colonizing days when Christendom's power was used to take over others' cultural territory. No, we can expect to be evangelized just as much as we ourselves evangelize.[4]

Mission, spirituality and English culture

I have already pointed out that John Drane is convinced that the English Church has to recover its own spiritual heart (for which there is a very long and deep tradition (Mursell, 2001)) if it is to re-engage with people outside itself today, and part

---

[4] For a critique of our inherited approach to evangelism and an explication of a non-violent and non-colonizing evangelism in our current era, see Bryan Stone, *Evangelism after Christendom: The Theology and Practice of Christian Witness* (Grand Rapids, MI: Brazos, 2007).

of this recovery for me has to be finding the spirituality that is already present 'out there'. It was interesting in the last chapter to note how, from the starting point of an English cultural saying, the reflection groups on occasion ended up in silence and contemplation. Holding a holy silence before our own culture as part of the process of listening to it would be a good start.

Many Christians and others (Moreton among them) want to write off the now well-known statistic referred to earlier in the book that around 70 per cent of people in England, when asked in the 2001 census, identified themselves as Christian. It will be interesting to see how that figure changes in the next census, but other surveys have roughly confirmed it throughout the first decade of the new century. The question is, does it mean anything? Are people defining themselves negatively? In other words, are they saying they are simply not Muslim or Hindu or atheist and that therefore their default position must be Christian still, although there is no real positive content to it? Certainly, Davie's 'believing without belonging' thesis is borne out when this percentage is compared with the church-going population of rarely more than 10 per cent.

It would be surprising however if these people did not have the capacity for spirituality, and other well-known research shows that, along with the decline in religiosity in this country, there has been an increase in personal spiritual awareness and experience when compared with an earlier similar study (Hay and Hunt, 2000). So perhaps if we were simply to take people's affirmation of their Christian faith at face value, as a measure of their openness to dealing with spirituality, we would be given another helpful starting point for our mission. But first let's remember that it may have been so for many centuries.

In *The Cloud of Unknowing*, a work in the English classic mystical tradition, the anonymous fourteenth-century author describes four 'levels' of Christian – Ordinary, Special, Solitary and Perfect. In order to move from one to the other, there needs to be a 'kindling of desire and fastened to it a leash of longing' (2001, p. 20). If the 70 per cent are 'ordinary' Christians, then the question is how do we kindle that desire in them – especially given the words of the Servant Song in Isaiah, which reminds us, 'A bruised reed he will not break, and a smouldering wick he will not snuff out' (Isa. 42.3, NIV).

First, as I remarked in an earlier chapter, we need to take utterly seriously (with Bediako and others writing from the African perspective) our 'primal' religion. This may go back as far as paganism and its current manifestation today, but also needs to include what has been known as 'folk religion' or more properly, when it is studied academically, *implicit religion* (see <www.implicitreligion.org>). Fair enough (as the English say), we could expect, along with Jeremy Paxman, that such belief would be even more 'temporizing, pliable and undogmatic' (1999, p. 95) than the religion he accuses the Church of England of holding. Nevertheless it is a starting point. We noted when studying the Robin Hood legends how, particularly in the early ballads, Robin and his band exemplify a lay Christianity which sits very lightly with organized religion, and perhaps not unreasonably so. Moreton thinks that if there is any hope for the Church of England, it is precisely because it has at least the possibility of coping at this starting point. He cites the example of the life and death of Jade Goody, a product of recent reality TV and celebrity culture (2010, pp. 313–18), and how she was baptized near her tragic death, praising the way her funeral was conducted and describing the sermon as 'brilliant'. As Moreton notes, 'this was the Church as servant, willing to offer a place for ritual and reflection to those in need'. Commenting on Moreton's book, the Bishop of Buckingham, Alan Wilson, supports this embrace of the inchoate faith of many English people:[5]

> Many of the people I served [when ministering in a parish], Churchgoing or not, were far wiser, more loving, courageous human beings than I'll ever be, and their general spiritual instinct to prioritise the Good Samaritan . . . was, in the main, sounder than any of us knew at the time.

---

[5] <http://bishopalan.blogspot.com/2010/05/god-not-englishman-official.html>, accessed 23 August 2010.

119

Perhaps the best example of theological reflection on this innate spirituality, even religiosity, of the English is a book of essays published by the Littlemore Group, theologians who are committed to doing academic theology while remaining rooted in ordinary life – sometimes in very difficult places. *Praying for England: Priestly Presence in Contemporary Culture* (Wells and Coakley, eds, 2008) deals with a diverse range of subjects, from an horrific murder to football and to finding just the right hymn to sing at a young person's funeral.

What then might we do practically to engage with this innate English spirituality, sense of fairness and desire for a better life? The short course on Englishness associated with this book could easily be adapted for use with any group of people in that 70 per cent band. In fact, while it hasn't been possible before the deadline for publication of this book, an army chaplain colleague of mine has plans to run the course with his soldiers in the near future. There is no reason why it might not be run in adult education centres or other neutral venues. The only change necessary would probably be for the facilitator to select a Bible passage to lay alongside the saying rather than allowing the group to choose their own, since the participants may not have that knowledge.

Another colleague, Paul Griffiths, has created some very interesting resources for engaging people outside the Church (<http://www.paulgriffithsministries.org.uk>). Not necessarily designed as a means to some future evangelization, they can stand alone and offer something to 'further humanity' among the participants. The first is an eight-week course engaging with the book *The Eight Secrets of Happiness* (Oxford: Lion Hudson, 2009), which addresses issues common to everyone – such as where to find joy, how to cope with stress and how to use time wisely (yes, we do have wisdom to offer here!). In a further application, various groups around the UK are working to stimulate public conversations on what makes for 'community well-being and personal happiness'. The idea is simple: in any local area, individuals from the worlds of politics, education, health, economics and the faith community are invited to chat before an invited audience about what they think will create greater community and personal happiness.

Then there is 'Table Talk' – another simple idea that employs a set of cards bearing themed questions on a variety of topics to get a conversation going in a pub or other 'safe space'. Remember how we have discovered that one contribution the Christian Church can make to Englishness is to move us from our basic social dis-ease and enable us to be much more face to face and eye to eye. This resource certainly works on that basis, as it asks questions like: How can I live a balanced life? How do you make and keep friends? How do we live a meaningful life? How do we care for the planet? How can we experience God?

Speaking of caring for the planet takes us to a second potentially fruitful area for our missional engagement today. It is no surprise that creation care has risen on to the mission agenda of the churches in recent years to an extent that, for example, it is now the fifth mark of authentic Anglican mission (to strive to safeguard the integrity of creation and sustain and renew the life of the earth), taking an equal place alongside proclaiming, teaching, baptizing, etc.[6] It is interesting that the only other sign of hope for the Church of England that Moreton identifies alongside the breadth of embrace offered to Jade Goody comes from TV personality and self-supporting priest Peter Owen-Jones, whom he meets in his parish of Firle in Sussex. Owen-Jones, on the back of his explorations for the BBC in world religion, thinks that 'a new manner of approaching nature and the divine is coming up through the earth', and that it is 'going to be the defining feature of the next fifty years' (Moreton, 2010, p. 332). Redemption, he claims, will no longer be a matter of saving the soul so much as the far more tangible task for people today of saving the planet we live on.

Tim Gorringe, Professor of Theology at the University of Exeter (whose book I referred to in depth in Chapter 1), is at the

---

[6] For an explication of the theology and practicalities of creation care, see the two sections under Mark 5 in Andrew Walls and Cathy Ross (eds), *Mission in the 21st Century: Exploring the Five Marks of Global Mission* (London: DLT, 2008, pp. 84–104).

forefront of research into the relationship between Christian churches and the Transition Town movement, which itself began in Devon (<http://www.transitionnetwork.org>). Transition towns are about being able to respond to 'peak oil' (the point when there is less oil left in the ground than we have already extracted, after which the price of fuel for transporting food will skyrocket) and climate change by sourcing all our food locally. My own experience is that there is some kind of movement developing on the ground,[7] to which I make my own small contribution by spending most of my days off growing vegetables on my inner-city allotment and trying (not very successfully at the moment) to keep poultry with a small group of other people.

And yet, is this such a new thing? It was pointed out more than once during our Englishness courses that part of English folk belief is identified in the fourth of five verses in the poem 'God's Garden' by Dorothy Gurney (1858–1932):

> The kiss of the sun for pardon,
>   The song of the birds for mirth,
> One is nearer God's heart in a garden,
>   Than anywhere else on earth.

It is a remarkable sentiment, given that Mrs Gurney was the daughter of one Anglican clergyman and then married another, she and her husband both becoming Roman Catholics eventually. You are nearer to God in a garden than in any church, or even during the Eucharist! Looked at in this way, the verse is taken a little out of the context of the whole poem (the first verse starts in Eden and the final one finishes in Gethsemane), but it has become ubiquitous in gardens all over the country. I remember I passed a version in a rock garden every day I walked to my primary school – it might have been one of the first things I learnt to read. It isn't a big step to make from looking for God in a garden to actively offering opportunities for others

---

[7] Another example would be the combination of environmentalism and new monasticism in Earth Abbey (<http://www.earthabbey.com>), which also runs co-operatives of people helping out in each other's gardens – they call the scheme 'Grow Zones'.

to do so, and this is the vision of the Quiet Garden movement (<www.quietgarden.co.uk>): 'to initiate and resource a network of local opportunities for prayer, silence, reflection and the appreciation of beauty; for learning about Christian spirituality; and for experiencing creativity and healing in the context of God's love'.

Towards a 'particular' English Church?

In this section I should like to pick up some of the ideas generated in the previous chapter and suggest future directions or experiments that others might like to take up. The point is to consciously engage our churches with Englishness in such a way that it actually becomes noticeable to the population.

Jeremy Paxman concurs that we are, for all the fudging of the Reformation in England, a peculiarly wordy culture as a result of it. He laments the amount of art (presumably Christian art) that was destroyed in favour of words in the sixteenth century and beyond (1999, p. 97). A recent visit to Venice reinforced this for me – if, prior to the Reformation, England had even a tenth of the art on display there, that still would have been a lot of art! Can we make any kind of a recovery here? Is there a vision of an English Christ we can identify with today that isn't a throwback to a previous age? We have public art in the Angel of the North and now a huge white horse to be erected in the south, for the Millennium we had Mark Wallinger's *Ecce Homo* on the fourth Trafalgar Square plinth, but what might the English Christ look like today?

We have learnt the fundamental importance of humour for the English, but it is probably more difficult to apply this insight than we might think. Our humour is subtle and often hidden away, under the surface, so I'm not sure Moreton's pagans have it quite right when they blow raspberries and shout out rude things during their rituals (2010, p. 335). Perhaps the best example of humour commending the faith, at least on our national public service broadcaster, the BBC, occurs not in the rather odd rural idyll of *The Vicar of Dibley* but in a more recent series set in inner-city London – *Rev*. Here there is a lot of humour, but also pathos and serious engagement with the problems of belief in such a setting. Clowning also might provide an interesting outlet for the subtleties of humour; there is something funny and scary about clowns, at the same time as they connect us with the importance of our own foolishness. Olive Drane <http://www.olivedrane.com> has been developing her own clown, Valentine, for more than twenty years. Then we have the satirical Christian website Ship of Fools (<www.shipoffools.com>) and Christian stand-up comics, but these seem to operate mostly within the Church or its subcultures. The question is, how can humour become part of the life and mission of the faith?

Virtually anyone who writes about the future of the Church speaks of the importance of creating community – a place where relationships can be nurtured and growth in wholeness and humanity can take place. This resonates with what we learnt about a Christian approach to the English home, where at best it offers security and safety as a basis for fellowship and engagement with the outside. One of the most interesting missional phenomena of recent times has been the rise of what is called new monasticism, a movement of people forming, under a 'rule of life', communities that nevertheless have a home base and a missional purpose. A good example of the many that have sprung up is the Northumbria Community (see <http://www.northumbriacommunity.org>). A constant challenge for local churches is how they can incorporate insights from these places into their ongoing life.

It is probably a matter for repentance that the Church of England has never truly engaged with the English hypocrisy we have discovered over the question of class. Paxman realizes that the C of E did not merely lose the cities and therefore the working class, it never had them, despite the huge Victorian church-building programme, the legacy of which we are left with today (1999, p. 107). Perhaps all we can do as a start is take class into account when engaging outside the Church. I was pleased to pick up recently an introductory course to the Christian faith which wasn't 12 weeks long and didn't require quite a lot of prior understanding. No, the videos were set in Blackpool – on the beach, up the Tower, in amusement arcades – and included vox pops on the Golden Mile from just the sort of people you would meet there. And once people from working-class backgrounds join the Church, can they be helped to become ministers and missionaries as 'indigenous' people to their own communities without being homogenized into some 'social base line uniformity' through the training process (Williams, 2009, p. 134)?

What would our worship look like if it took Englishness seriously? In other cultures, particularly in the Roman Catholic Church, it is very important that inculturation cashes out in the liturgy – especially the Eucharist. What would an English eucharistic prayer look like? Is there an expert liturgist out there who might have a go at writing one? It needn't be used every week, but it might be brought out on special occasions like St George's Day (more of which in a moment). And what of our preaching? I recently came across an interesting book from America (Cosgrove and Edgerton, 2007) which argues for 'incarnational translation in preaching'. Taking the insights from Bible translation and hermeneutics that I referred to in Chapter 3, they show how the texts of Scripture can be made to live in local and particular contexts.

To me, the most obvious implication of this study for our theological institutions is that they should begin to teach social anthropology in some depth. The subject has been essential in the formation of missionaries for some decades, as it is the discipline which enables *deep listening* to the community in which the missioner is set. The Americans have led the way here, with Charles Kraft (1996) and Paul Hiebert (2008) being two key authors in the field. *Partnership for Missional Church*, a programme of adaptive change management for local churches created by Pat Kiefert (<http://www.churchinnovations.org>), utilizes these insights such that any lay person can take them up.

Once the church, along with the academy, begins to take the task of deep listening to culture and place seriously, we might begin to generate a corpus of English contextual theology that provides a resource for our mission. I offer this book as a contribution to that process.

Celebrating our Christianity in English ways

I close with some wisdom from my colleague Helen Cameron, who directs research at the Oxford Centre for Ecclesiology and Practical Theology. She has suggested that we in our post-Christendom world would do well to learn from the Eastern faiths, which place an emphasis on three elements of religious practice that have rather fallen out of use among us since the Reformation. Here are some concluding ideas, focusing on shrines, festivals and pilgrimage, as to how we might celebrate our Englishness, history and tradition.

Shrine

I came across a Baptist church recently that, rarely for churches belonging to this denomination, had its baptistery in the street outside the church. This was because the village was originally Nonconformist and the Baptists pre-dated the arrival of the Anglicans by several decades. Some time ago the congregation had moved out of their small church into a school for worship and the baptistery hadn't been used for years. When they went out to do their deep listening in the community, what the members of the congregation heard was the concern of village people about the neglect of the baptistery. So they planned to restore it to its former glory and possibly use it again. A small example of how important 'shrines' can be to us all, resonant of our identity as they are.

A shrine is a holy place – a place which points us to the other, to heaven, but which is rooted in our particular history and tradition. We neglect such places at our peril. On a much larger scale, Glastonbury was once our national shrine, but I do not get much sense that its faith potential is realized today. All we hear of is the annual rock festival and how the spiritual searchers have moved in.

No doubt many other sites have strong local significance that could be recovered (especially given the size of the book *England in Particular* (Clifford and King, 2006)) – but that is not all that is required. For what happens at the shrines of other religions is that once you are there, there is an opportunity to offer some devotion. So it should be possible at such sites to light a candle, or to say, write or leave a prayer – and probably even to meet someone face to face.

Festival

The obvious festival that we are missing out on – and probably giving over to the racists – is St George's Day. We noted earlier how the Archbishop of York has called for more engagement with it (Sentamu, 2009), even asking for it to become a national holiday. While in some localities the church bells have been rung in the morning of St George's Day, it would be great to see churches getting out on to the streets to celebrate; if we had the day off, so much the better. And, as I suggested earlier, what better day to celebrate a new English liturgy?

There are lots of other festivals though, and it's no surprise that the pagans make a lot of the seasonal festivals. As Moreton points out (2010, p. 299), what we tend to hear from Christians about these is rather negative – 'We're not celebrating Hallowe'en, which even if it is right does not send a good message, and Christmas – well, it's over-commercialized, but do come to church, even if it's only for that rather anonymous carol service.' What about putting on an English nativity play, like *Joe Carpenter & Son* (Clarke, 1990), that isn't just for children and involves the whole community – again, bringing people together face to face? Or reviving Robin Hood celebrations in May? It would make a change from the average village fete or summer fair.

Pilgrimage

Pilgrimage is already making a comeback, as anyone who has been on the route to Santiago de Compostela in Spain knows. And many Christians will tell you that it never went away, as they go on their annual pilgrimage to the shrine (yes, that idea again) at Walsingham in Norfolk. Here of course the three ideas can come together; it is possible to take a pilgrimage to a shrine and then have a festival when you get there. The reason pilgrimage 'works' is that it offers a space where masks and defences can come down, class differences are left at home and deep human interaction can take place. Some years ago I was involved in the development of a new pilgrimage route from Leicester to Lincoln in the East Midlands, which we called St Hugh's Way. And other new routes are springing up around the country – for instance the new St Chad's Way from Chester to Lichfield (see <http://www.stchadsstafford.co.uk/page.asp?pid=60>).

No doubt there are many other possibilities of combinations of these three elements. I have just attended the annual Greenbelt festival at Cheltenham, which strikes me as the most open (to the outsider) and missional of all the Christian festivals, although all combine elements of pilgrimage.

I could go on. But my final point here is to hand the task of continuing the English inculturation project over to you, the reader, in the hope that together we can continue to realize the integration of Christ and culture in our blessed plot.

Appendix

How can we be English and Christian? An imaginative and reflective course integrating Englishness and Christian faith

---

Introduction

What follows is an abridged version of the Englishness course 'facilitator's handbook', which, if you wish to run it, is available in full at <www.spckpublishing.co.uk/shop/the-faith-of-the-english> along with a handout to give to participants. Downloading it should help you to prepare for and deliver the course in your own way, enabling you to become familiar with and adapt the process for your own context without having to keep referring to the back of this book for guidance.

Nevertheless we thought it would be helpful to reproduce the course in some detail in the book, so that readers can weigh up whether or not they would like to offer it themselves and also connect it with the relevant chapters in the book. It is not necessary to have read the book in its entirety before attempting to run the course – it stands alone as an adult theological education course in its own right.

Why this course?

There was a time in the not so distant past when it was thought that to be Christian and English were virtually the same thing. We exported our faith around the world along with quite a bit of our culture – but we weren't aware of how embedded our culture was in our faith. This is no longer the case. Although many people in England tick the 'Christian' box on the national census, only a small percentage actually profess and act on the Christian faith, believing that it can make a difference to, even transform their lives. In addition, other cultures and other faiths are present in many of our towns and cities, so we cannot simply equate our culture and our faith any more. All this leaves us with a question which may not have been asked in our land for centuries: how can we be English *and* Christian?

A very similar question is asked in many parts of the world today by people from all sorts of ethnic and language groups who have become Christian more recently – especially if they have inherited their Christian faith from Western Christians. How can we be Masai or Tamil or Native American *and* Christian?

This question is an urgent one for English people who are Christians – one that we need to begin to answer for several reasons:

- Unless we are sure of our identity, we cannot easily deal with the 'other', or what the Bible calls the 'stranger in our midst'. Without such knowledge it is easy to be quickly threatened by outsiders or those with a different identity.
- Perhaps we feel a little bit embarrassed about our Englishness – but in conversation (or should we say dialogue?) with the good news of the Christian faith, we may find some things – perhaps many – that are blessed with through being English.
- In this way we might come to know, when we meet our sisters and brothers from other cultures, what is our contribution to world Christianity.
- Englishness is on the agenda of many in our society today, and not always for good reasons; some people want to emphasize their English identity as distinct from people from other ethnic backgrounds. Therefore we might also find aspects of Englishness that need to be transformed by the gospel, and others that need to be discarded, if that were possible.
- Most of all, as Christians, we need to be aware of culture – of its blessings and curses – in order to live well in our world today and to become better human beings in the process.
- Finally, a clearer understanding of our Englishness may be helpful for our mission in England. If we know who we are and why, and where we are blessed by the gospel, perhaps we will be more ready and better equipped to share that new, better Englishness with others.

Who is involved?

Adult theological education courses are delivered in all sorts of ways, by all sorts of people. Perhaps the best way is in small groups.

Conventional wisdom about group size says that they shouldn't consist of fewer than 6 or 7 people or more than 15, but between 8 and 12 is best.

Obviously it is important that the vast majority of participants are English or can identify themselves as English in some way, no matter what their ethnic background. It might be interesting if one of the facilitators was not English. If there are people who would not consider themselves to be English but would like to join the course, they could join in the reflections if they felt able – or they could take up the role of observer(s) to the process and offer their own perspectives as an 'outsider' from time to time, especially in the middle and at the end.

Each group needs a facilitator, or preferably two. Having two facilitators can introduce balance in the leadership both in style and gender and leaves a backup if one can't make a session. It also means there is someone available (other than group participants) to record on flip charts the material generated, which is an important part of the process.

What will you need?

The six sessions are as follows:

1 Moderation: 'Don't rock the boat'
2 Humorous moaning: 'Typical!'
3 Privacy: 'An Englishman's home is his castle'
4 Fair play: 'Well, to be fair . . .'
5 Class: 'I know my place'
6 Courtesy: 'Sorry!'

You will need two flip charts and flip-chart paper and plenty of pens for the facilitator, as a lot of material is collected from the group on the charts during each session. Something (Blu-tack® or masking tape) to stick up the flip chart sheets as they are generated is also required. Someone should be responsible for organizing and resourcing these materials.

It will also be helpful if some in the group have access to computers and the internet as there will be a task to be undertaken between the sessions which will build up to the end of the course. The resources available on the internet will be invaluable for this. If this is not possible, the facilitators should get hold of a copy of the CMS/USPG

Christ We Share pack, which contains pictures of Christ from around the world. (Published in 2000, it is still available from the USPG online shop.)

When should you meet?

As you can see, the course includes enough material for six sessions, with an option for a seventh if the group feel it necessary. The six sessions could, for instance, fit into the six weeks of Lent, although the last session may then fall in Holy Week. (It could of course be run at any other time as well.) The course is designed to be flexible, but facilitators will need to plan in good time what will happen and when.

Our method

Each week will follow a similar pattern and will use a method based on an imaginative way of doing theological reflection.[1] The material is dependent on a serious in-depth study of 'the English' by Kate Fox, published in 2004 as *Watching the English: The Hidden Rules of English Behaviour.* Fox studied Englishness for three years using a method anthropologists call 'participant observation'. There is no need to worry about what this is now or even read her book (but it is a very readable and accessible book and would be a good way to follow up the course).

Fox identifies ten characteristics of Englishness which she feels are unique. This course reduces the ten characteristics to six, as some of them overlap and six seems a manageable number of sessions! Each characteristic described by Fox has become associated with a common saying or proverb, and it is from these sayings that our reflections will start. Each session begins and ends with prayer and worship. it is important that the course is more than just an intellectual exercise but something that will affect all of us – body, mind *and* spirit.

There are suggested timings for the various parts of the session, assuming a duration for the meeting of two hours. You may want to advertise the sessions as being 2½ hours long in order to allow plenty

---

[1] The method has been modified for our purposes but is based on one widely used in the course *Education for Ministry*, a four-year course which explores the Old Testament, the New Testament, Church History and Theology alongside theological reflections of the kind used in this course. Any participants interested in exploring it further should look at <www.efmuk.org.uk> – it is highly recommended.

of time for meeting up, and for refreshments at some appropriate point (in the middle, between stages of the reflection) and also a little leeway should the discussion go on longer.

Getting started

Since the group will be forming in the first session, it's important in this session that the facilitators lead the opening and closing prayers – but then ask if others are willing to share this task in future weeks (see below).

When choosing the passages from Scripture or tradition, I have suggested some possibilities each week but it may be best to free the group to choose their own. Some groups will be better at this than others, and will pick the idea up more quickly. It is worth noting, however, that if the group does choose its own passage, it tends to take longer and can be controversial!

It would also be good to encourage group members to begin thinking about the theme for the following week during the days before the group session. In this way they may access their stories about the theme more quickly.

During the sessions 'insights and ideas' might be offered by participants at any time. These need to be captured on a flip chart so they can be reviewed near the end of the session. Participants also need to be encouraged by facilitators to offer them at any stage – as soon as they come. The insights might be quite varied; do encourage those that are on the theme of Englishness and the Christian faith.

Note for the reader:
The six sessions of the course are outlined below. The first session is laid out in full, including timings; after that, since there is a general repetition of the process, only the section headings with a brief explanation are given. Any deviation from the 'norm' is explained in full. The complete version of the course can be found on the SPCK website at the address given above.

Week 1: Moderation: 'Don't rock the boat'

Opening activity and prayer [10 mins]

Lay out a selection of pictures or words of English 'icons' (or key images which have a deep meaning for us – like postboxes or robins or Big Ben) for the group and ask everyone to choose one that attracts them.[2] Then ask each member of the group to share why they have chosen that particular icon and to introduce themselves to other group members (ask them to take about a minute each).

You may then want to offer an opening prayer.

A prayer of Wulfstan, monk and Bishop of Worcester (*c.*1009–95) [slightly adapted]

O Lord have mercy on us sinners. Establish our hearts in your will. Grant us true repentance for our sins: right faith and true charity, patience in adversity and moderation in prosperity. Help us and our friends and kinsmen. Show mercy to all who have done us good and shown us the knowledge of good, and grant everlasting forgiveness to all who have spoken or thought evil against us. To you our God, and to all your holy ones, be praise and glory for ever for all the benefits you have given us, and for all your mercies to us sinners: for your name's sake. Amen.

Reflection

Moderation, says Kate Fox (who was referred to in the introduction), is a deep-seated English reflex – or default mode. I am not sure if you watch reality TV shows, but it's always interesting to see whom the public choose to win these shows. Very often it isn't the most extreme or the loudest people who are chosen, but rather the average types, the ones who probably sit on the fence and 'don't rock the boat'.

It seems that the English most often go for the middle ground, not liking extremes of any kind. This is true of politics: the Labour party could only be elected in the 1990s by moving back to the centre from the left. Is it any surprise then that one of the key values in Anglicanism – our national Church – is the middle way between different extremes?

So the starting point for our first reflection is the common English saying, 'Don't rock the boat'.

---

[2] Examples of the English icons used at the start of the first session can be viewed at <http://www.icons.org.uk/>, and you could pick up pictorial versions of them from newspapers and magazines or other websites. (They cannot be downloaded from that particular website because they are in copyright.) You may also want to obtain a copy or version of Holman Hunt's *The Light of the World* for the closing meditation in the first session.

1 Creating a cultural world

Draw a circle in the middle of a flip-chart sheet and write the saying in the middle of the circle. Then divide the sheet up into four parts from the centre.

Ask the group to imagine a world where the saying 'Don't rock the boat' is the defining principle. Then ask four sets of questions about this imaginary world:

1 What is a world defined by 'Don't rock the boat' like? What does it feel like? What would it be like to live permanently in that world?
2 What is good and true about life in that world?
3 What would make the world defined by 'Don't rock the boat' a better place – what would have to change? What, if anything, might be left behind or let go of?
4 What's the best possible picture we could have of this world? Or, to put it another way, what would be a reason for a big party in this world?

Take each question in turn and fill in the quadrants on the flip chart with the group's answers. Try to take as many answers as possible – there are no right or wrong ones.

[20 mins – 5 mins per question/quadrant]

When you have finished, stick the flip-chart sheet on a wall so that it is visible.

2 Relating to the tradition

The group should now take up to five minutes to generate passages from the Bible or other elements of the Christian tradition (the lives of saints or modern Christian 'heroes' for instance) which *resonate* or chime with 'Don't rock the boat'. It is best if a short extract or sentence is chosen which sums up the passage. These should be listed on the flip chart.

The group should then reflect together for a further five minutes on which passage best matches the saying 'Don't rock the boat'. Note that this isn't about finding some verse or passage that's *exactly* equivalent to the ideas in 'Don't rock the boat', but something that can be placed fruitfully alongside it that it evokes, or as I said earlier, that resonates with it. So it might be tempting (and possibly fruitful) here to choose one of the stories about Jesus in a boat in a storm, but what about when the Gerasene men 'beg Jesus to leave the district' after their pigs have rushed off to be drowned in Mark 5.17? They have certainly had their 'boat rocked' and they don't like it!

When the group has brainstormed ideas, decide on one piece of Scripture or tradition to use. Focus on a particular idea or phrase that sums it up (e.g. 'they begged Jesus to leave the district', as above) and write it in the centre of a new flip-chart sheet.
[10 mins max for this whole section]

3 Creating a world from the tradition

Draw the four quadrants again and then ask similar questions to those above – but now of the world created by this new phrase, sentence or idea.

1 What is this world like? What does it feel like? What would it be like to live permanently in this world?
2 What is good and true about life in this world?
3 What would make this world a better place – what would have to change? What, if anything, might be left behind or let go of?
4 What's the best possible picture we could have of this world? Or, to put it another way, what would be a reason for a big party in this world?

[20 mins – 5 mins per quadrant]

4 Comparing and contrasting the worlds

Once this flip chart is complete, place it alongside the one with 'Don't rock the boat' at the centre. Now compare and contrast the four quadrants. What similarities and differences emerge? Write these up on another chart. From this point it may be that insights start emerging for the group. Remember to encourage these and write them up on a separate sheet of paper.
[10 mins]

There are three further stages, the first of which may be left out if there is little time remaining.

5 Telling our stories

Organize the group into pairs and ask them to share quickly with each other a short episode from their experience that is evoked in their memory by the phrase 'Don't rock the boat'. Two or three participants

who feel able to do so can share their story with the whole group.
Remember that insights and new ideas might emerge here too.
[15 mins]

6 Taking positions

Give everyone five minutes in quiet to prepare a 'position statement'
from their own interaction with the reflection. Each person needs to
develop a single short sentence beginning with the words

I believe that . . .

or

I think that . . .

Now air these in the group in turn and write them up on the flip
chart. Once everyone has given their statement, see if any more
insights have emerged.
[20 mins]

7 Taking action

Again each person should spend a few minutes in silence, this time
thinking what action, if any, they might take as a result of the reflection.
For instance, it might affect relationships, family life or decisions that
have to be made. Some of these ideas can be shared in the group.
[15 mins]

Closing prayer

Spend some moments in quiet and then offer to God the positions
and actions taken up by the group. Or show Holman Hunt's picture
of Christ, *The Light of the World*, and reflect on it and the themes of
the evening.
[5 mins]

Optional homework: The iconic 'English' Christ

If the group would like to spend a small amount of time between
meetings investigating the themes further, there is an optional piece
of work they could do.

Individually, or in small groups of two or three (depending on the
size of the whole group), share out the next five weeks between

everyone. Each person or group should research and prepare a short closing meditation for the end of the session for their designated week. [If the group decides not to do this it will be for the facilitator(s) to prepare something appropriate for the end of each session.]

The group will imagine they are sharing reflections on the 'English Christ' for a group of overseas visitors. This can be done by means of pictures, music or poetry, or any other medium – but it should be meditative and prayerful. If it were also to pick up the theme of that particular week's meeting that would be an added bonus. The facilitators could offer to take the first two weeks' closing meditations if it was felt there was not enough time for group members to prepare.

The optional exercise could be introduced to the group by showing some pictures of Jesus from around the world. A range of such images can be found in the CMS/USPG *Christ We Share* pack mentioned in the introduction, or there are some available at <http://www.rejesus.co.uk/expressions/faces_jesus/index.html>.

The key question in this exercise is how can Christ be portrayed to the English. Is it as Holman Hunt's *The Light of the World* (as shown on the above website) or are there other more interesting, radical or engaging ways of portraying Christ through English culture?

Week 2: Humorous moaning: 'Typical!'

Opening activity and prayer

Talk about the weather. This should be easy for the group! Which types of weather do members like best? Which seasons are preferable? Why does it always rain at weekends? What does it do to our spirits to be always wishing it was warmer when it's cold and cooler when it's hot?

Needless to say, the Anglican Book of Common Prayer from 1662 has two weather prayers, one 'For Rain' and another 'For fair Weather' (and Weather here really does have a capital letter, because of course there is either too much or too little of it!). While drought and flooding are very serious matters for those they affect, even today, it might be worth thinking about whether we can best respond to them with humour or prayer (or both?). We can pray one or both of these prayers now:

O God, heavenly Father, who by thy Son Jesus Christ hast promised to all them that seek thy kingdom, and the righteousness thereof, all things necessary to their bodily sustenance; Send us, we beseech thee, in this our necessity, such moderate rain and showers, that we may receive the fruits of the earth to our comfort, and to thy honour; through Jesus Christ our Lord. Amen.

O Almighty Lord God, who for the sin of man didst once drown all the world, except eight persons, and afterward of thy great mercy didst promise never so to destroy it again; We humbly beseech thee, that although we for our iniquities have worthily deserved a plague of rain and waters, yet upon such true repentance thou wilt send us such weather, as that we may receive the fruits of the earth in due season; and learn both by thy punishment to amend our lives, and for thy clemency to give thee praise and glory; through Jesus Christ our Lord. Amen.

Reflection

This week we are combining (because I think they go together and overlap) two of Kate Fox's ideas about us as the English. While the English have no monopoly on humour, in her book Fox writes that what is unique about us is the 'sheer pervasiveness and supreme importance of humour in English everyday life and culture . . . It is our "default mode"; it is like breathing, we cannot function without it.' And within and beneath this humour is that tendency to moaning, which Kate calls (in her own humorous English way) 'Eeyorishness' – after the rather sad but enduring donkey character in the quintessentially English *Winnie the Pooh* stories by A. A. Milne. This is 'our chronic pessimism, our assumption that it is in the nature of things to go wrong and be disappointing, but also our perverse satisfaction at seeing our gloomy predictions fulfilled'. So if we combine humour with Eeyorishness, we come to what Fox describes as one of our few national catchphrases . . . 'Typical!'

When you start listening out for this response to what life brings to us every day, it really is surprising how often you hear it. It rained again at the weekend . . . typical! The Government want to raise taxes, reorganize the Health Service, or in some new way interfere in our lives . . . typical! We choose the wrong queue in the supermarket – again! . . . typical!

Appendix

1 Telling our stories

Quieten the group for a few moments so that everyone can compose a short 'Typical!' story. It should be possible to convey it in about three sentences, finishing with the word 'typical!' For example:

> *Last week I booked to go to London on the train. I arrived at the station in really good time. But then I discovered the timetable had been changed . . . typical!*

2 Creating a cultural world

Draw a circle in the middle of a flip-chart sheet and write 'Typical!' in the middle of the circle. Then divide the sheet up into four parts from the centre.

Like last week with 'Don't rock the boat', ask the group to imagine a world where 'typical' is the defining principle. Then ask the same four sets of questions about this imaginary world.

3 Relating to the tradition

The group should now take up to five minutes to generate passages from the Bible or other elements of the Christian tradition (the lives of saints or modern Christian 'heroes', for instance) which resonate or chime with 'Typical!' It is best if a short extract or sentence is chosen which sums up the passage. These are listed on the flip chart.

The group should then reflect together for a further five minutes on which passage best matches the saying 'Typical!' Again, remember this isn't about finding some verse or passage that's *exactly* equivalent to the ideas in 'Typical!', but something that can be placed fruitfully alongside it that it evokes, or that resonates with it. So it might be tempting (and possibly helpful) here to choose one of the stories about Jonah under his tree, where he accuses God of behaving typically and forgiving those awful Ninevehites. But what about the man who, when confronted by Jesus ('Do you want to be healed?', John 5.6, RSV), reckons he has been 'trying' to get healed for 38 years by the pool of Siloam, but 'someone else always gets in first'.

When the group has decided which piece of Scripture or tradition to use, they should focus on a single idea or phrase or short sentence, which is then written in the centre of a new flip-chart sheet.

4 Creating a world from the tradition

Draw the four quadrants again and then ask similar questions to those in Week 1.

5 Comparing and contrasting the worlds

Once this flip-chart sheet is complete, place it alongside the one with 'Typical!' at the centre. Now compare and contrast the four quadrants.

6 Taking positions

Allow everyone five minutes in quiet to prepare a 'position statement' from their own interaction with the reflection.

7 Taking action

Again, allow each person a few minutes to think what action, if any, they might take as a result of the study.

Closing meditation

Week 3: Privacy: 'An Englishman's home is his castle'

Opening activity and prayer

What surrounds your house – fence, wall or hedge? How high is it? How do you relate to your neighbours? Does anyone in the group live in a flat? What difference might that make?

Two English prayers

> Lord Jesus, come quickly; my heart is desirous of thy presence, and would entertain thee, not as a guest, but as an inhabitant, as the Lord of all my faculties. Enter in and take possession, and dwell with me for ever, that I also may dwell in the heart of my dearest Lord, which was opened for me with a spear and Love.
>
> Jeremy Taylor (1613–67)

> O almighty God, inspire us with this divine principle; kill in us all the seeds of envy and ill-will; and help us, by cultivating within ourselves the love of neighbour, to improve in the love of thee. Thou hast placed us in various kindreds, friendships, and relations, as the school of discipleship for our

affections: help us, by the due exercise of them, to improve to perfection; till all partial affection be lost in that universal one, and thou, O God, shalt be all in all. Amen.

Joseph Butler (1692–1752)

Reflection

This week we come to what perhaps is the 'core' of Englishness. Kate Fox claims that as a nation we simply find social interaction very difficult. Interestingly she attributes both our well-known 'English reserve' and our less flattering, but equally well-known 'English hooliganism' as two sides of this same coin (you'll have to read her book to find how she comes to this conclusion). When out in public, then, we find ways around our awkwardness by talking about the weather, our pets, anything in fact which gets us into a conversation without too much threat. Therefore we are most at ease when in private. We feel at home when in our own surroundings and we value privacy in order be 'at home' – at ease. There is a deep connection in our culture between home and privacy.

It is this connection we are going to explore this week by using a saying which everyone will be familiar with: 'An Englishman's home is his castle'. Of course we are not just referring to English *men* this week – the saying is meant to include women as well, it's just that it was coined before we became used to using inclusive language. We could say that for English folk their home is their castle – but somehow it doesn't sound quite the same.

Anyway, what's important about the saying is the metaphor implied within it: that in some way for us we treat *home* as *castle*.

1 Creating a cultural world

Draw a circle in the middle of a flip-chart sheet and write the saying in the middle of the circle. Then divide the sheet up into four parts from the centre. Next, ask the usual four sets of questions of this world where home is like a castle.

2 Relating to the tradition

Take up to five minutes to generate passages from the Bible or other pieces of the Christian tradition that resonate with 'home as castle'. It is best if a short extract or sentence is chosen which sums up the passage. These are listed on the flip chart.

The group should then reflect together for a further five minutes on which passage best matches the saying 'An Englishman's home is his castle'. We are looking for something that can be placed fruitfully alongside it that it evokes, or that resonates with it. One possibility might be when the disciples are locked in the upper room after the crucifixion and the Risen Jesus comes and meets them (John 20.19). Another might be when the Jewish exiles in Babylon are told to bless the city of their travail by building houses and living in them (Jer. 29.5).

When the group has decided which piece of Scripture or tradition to use, they should focus on a single idea or phrase or short sentence. This is then written in the centre of a new flip-chart sheet.

3 Creating a world from the tradition

Draw the four quadrants again and then ask similar questions to those above – but now of the world created by this new phrase, sentence or idea.

4 Comparing and contrasting the worlds

Once this flip chart is complete, place it alongside the one with 'home as castle' at the centre. Now compare and contrast the four quadrants.

5 Telling our stories

Organize the group into pairs and ask them to share quickly with each other a short episode from their experience that is evoked in their memory by the saying, 'An Englishman's home is his castle'.

6 Taking positions

Allow everyone five minutes in quiet to prepare a 'position statement' from their own interaction with the reflection.

7 Taking action

Each person should again spend a few minutes thinking what action, if any, they might take as a result of the study.

Closing meditation

Week 4: Fair play: 'Well, to be fair...'

Opening activity and prayer

Ask the group why they think the English are famous for queuing. Ask if anyone has ever jumped a queue – or stopped someone else doing it. Explain that an experiment was done (by Kate Fox in *Watching the English*) to show that if you find a kiosk in a train or bus station at which there is no queue and stand about 15 to 20 feet away from it, pretty soon people will come up to you and ask 'Are you in the queue?'

Sir Jacob Astley prayed before the Battle of Edgehill in the English Civil War in 1642. Rather than pray for victory, or for defeat for the enemy, he used this rather beautiful prayer which probably only an Englishman could use before going into battle to face life or death. We can pray it now, too, as a prayer both for this session and for our lives, which can also be a bit 'busy'.

> Lord, help me today to realize that thou wilt be speaking to me
> Through the events of the day,
> through people, through things, and through all creation.
> Give me ears, eyes and heart to perceive thee,
> however veiled thy presence may be.
> Give me insight to see through the exterior of things
> to the interior truth.
> Give me the Spirit of discernment.
> O Lord, thou knowest how busy I must be this day.
> If I forget thee, do not thou forget me. Amen.

Reflection

How often do we hear the phrase 'Well, to be fair...'? We know how it is – things have to be equalled up over time. You bought a round in the pub last time, it's now my turn; guests are served first at the table; we say 'After you' when passing through a door. The English always like to support the underdog in any sporting contest, as well as being wary of too much success (originally, when logs were still sawn up by hand, the long saw was held between two men, one above and one below the log in a sawing pit. The underdog was the poor guy in the bottom of the pit – the one who spent all day literally spitting sawdust). And, since usually we are not expected to win, this suits us fine. In fact it sometimes seems that we don't start fully participating or playing the game until 'our backs are against the wall' and the 'Dunkirk spirit' re-emerges (for example, how many times have the England football team really only begun to play after one of the team is sent off?). This is all about the little guy standing up for what's fair – and it's why Robin Hood is one of our heroes, since what happened to him was so unfair.

Our sense of fairness becomes particularly apparent at Christmas – we agonize if someone has sent us a card or present and we haven't been able to respond. But it's not just about sport or Christmas this week because, as Kate Fox points out, fairness and fair play are at the root of much of our morality and, when placed alongside the value of moderation which we looked at in Week 1, we then show our capacity for moral tolerance, for compromise, for letting things be – 'letting sleeping dogs lie'.

It could be claimed that the undeserved love and grace that God offers us is very *unfair*. So this may be a very challenging week for us!

1 Telling our stories

As in Week 2, we are going to start this week by sharing stories, this time about fair play or fairness. It should not be difficult for participants to get in touch with times they felt that they or someone else was treated unfairly. But they should also think about what kind of incident or story from our lives could end up with the comment, 'Well, to be fair . . .'

Two or three participants who feel able to do so can share their stories with the whole group.

2 Creating a cultural world

Draw the circle as usual in the middle of a flip-chart sheet and write the saying in the middle of the circle. Ask the usual four questions for the world characterized by this saying.

3 Relating to the tradition

Take up to five minutes to generate passages from the Bible or other elements of the Christian tradition which resonate with 'Well, to be fair . . .' Choose short extracts or sentences which sum up the passage. List these on the flip chart.

The group should then reflect together for a further five minutes on which one best matches the saying 'Well, to be fair . . .' In this case it might be good to think about a passage where what happens does seem unfair. A classic example would be the elder brother in the parable of the Prodigal Son (Luke 15) – although some people think this should be called the parable of the Prodigal Father since he does some extremely unconventional and shocking things!

When the group has decided which piece of Scripture or tradition to use, they should focus on a single idea or phrase or short sentence, which is then written in the centre of a new flip-chart sheet.

4 Creating a world from the tradition

Draw the four quadrants again and then ask similar questions to those above – but now of the world created by this new phrase, sentence or idea.

5 Comparing and contrasting the worlds

Once this flip chart is complete, place it alongside the one with 'Well, to be fair . . .' at the centre. Now compare and contrast the four quadrants.

6 Taking positions

Allow everyone five minutes in quiet to prepare a 'position statement' from their own interaction with the reflection.

7 Taking action

Again, each person should spend a few minutes thinking what action, if any, they might take as a result of the study.

Closing meditation

Week 5: Class: 'I know my place'

Prayer and introductory activity

This week we start with a prayer which is taken from the Litany of Remembrance of George Ridding (1828–1904), first Bishop of Southwell. The full Litany touches on many of the themes of this course and is a thoroughly English piece of spiritual writing. We might want to ask who decides what 'true sense and taste' is and what offensive manners are, but probably it is worth praying it first . . .

> From self-conceit and vanity and boasting; from delight in sup-posed success and superiority, raise us to the modesty and humil-ity of true sense and taste and reality; and from all the harms and hindrances of offensive manners and self-assertion,
> Save us and help us, **we humbly beseech thee, O Lord.**

> From strife and partisanship and division among thy people, from magnifying our certainties to condemn all differences, from all arrogance in our dealings with others,
> Save us and help us, **we humbly beseech thee, O Lord.**

> Give us true knowledge of other people in their differences from us and in their likenesses to us, that we may deal with their real selves, measuring their feelings by our own, but patiently con-sidering their varied lives and thoughts and circumstances; and in all our relations to them, from false judgments of our own, from misplaced trust and distrust, from misplaced giving and refusing, from misplaced praise and rebuke,
> Save us and help us, **we humbly beseech thee, O Lord.**

Class is a very pervasive but also very sensitive issue in England, despite recent government announcements about the advent of a 'classless' society. This might be the most challenging session of all in this course. It's not something we often, if ever, talk about in church!

The clothes we wear, the school we went to, the way we talk, even what we call the bit of paper or cloth placed on a table for wiping our mouths and hands with after a meal – all are signals of what class we fit into. We are able, somehow, to effortlessly gauge the class of others without even saying a word to them.

This isn't quite the same thing as the classification developed every ten years in our national census. It's possible to earn lots of money but still be regarded by most people as in the 'lower' classes (e.g. some Premiership footballers), or to be quite poor financially but still be considered 'upper class' or 'posh'.

Reflection

There is a very simple way into this week's reflection and that is for the group to watch (perhaps on a laptop) a TV sketch from the 1960s featuring John Cleese, Ronnie Barker and Ronnie Corbett. There are several versions available on YouTube. The three men in the sketch stand in line and explain in turn what it is to be upper, middle and working class. Needless to say they all wear different clothes and have different accents. The very popularity of the sketch even today shows how current the issues it raises still are. The refrain, 'I know my place', which is repeated as the punchline, is spoken by Ronnie Corbett, the working-class character. Nevertheless it is clear that each character in a different way 'knows his place' in the class system – as we all instinctively do.

1 Telling our stories

Again, we need to tell our own stories first in order to get a feel for the saying we are working with. Honesty will be required here because we may not want to admit to too much class prejudice. It may help to start in pairs; ask each member of the group to share briefly with their partner a short episode from their experience that is evoked in their memory by the saying, 'I know my place'. Two or three participants who feel able to do so can share their stories with the whole group.

2 Creating a cultural world

Draw a circle as usual in the middle of a flip-chart sheet and write the saying, 'I know my place' in the middle of the circle. Divide the sheet up into four parts from the centre. We enter the world of the saying we have chosen by asking, as before, the four sets of questions.

3 Relating to the tradition

Take up to five minutes to generate passages from the Bible or other elements of the Christian tradition which resonate with the saying. It's best if a short extract or sentence is chosen which sums up the passage. List these on the flip chart.

The group should reflect together for a further five minutes on which passage best matches the saying. It might not be that easy this week to think up connective passages or pieces of tradition, so I am going to suggest one or two which might be helpful.

The life of William Carey (1761–1834), the founder of the Baptist Missionary Society in the late eighteenth and early nineteenth century, is a fascinating story of someone who started with working-class roots, but who by hard work, self-teaching and great faith did achieve amazing things in his life. Having started life as a cobbler, he worked in India as a missionary until the end of his life, learning and mastering several languages.

A story is told of when Carey was invited to dinner in India with the Marquis of Hastings and several army officers.[3] Someone turned to him and asked whether he had been a shoemaker, to which he replied: 'No, sir! only a cobbler' [i.e. a repairer of shoes]. So the group could use the phrase '*only* a cobbler' as the starting point for the second reflection.

Apparently when Carey was baptized (as an adult), the minister used the text 'Many that are first shall be last, and the last shall be first.' This too would be an appropriate piece of Scripture to reflect with.

When the group has decided which piece of Scripture or tradition to use, they should focus on a single idea or phrase or short sentence, which is then written in the centre of a new flip-chart sheet.

4 Creating a world from the tradition

Draw the four quadrants again and then ask similar questions to those above – but now of the world created by this new phrase, sentence or idea.

5 Comparing and contrasting the worlds

Once this flip chart is complete, place it alongside the earlier one. Compare and contrast the four quadrants.

6 Taking positions

Allow everyone five minutes in quiet to prepare a 'position statement' from their own interaction with the reflection.

7 Taking action

Again, allow each person a few minutes to think what action, if any, they might take as a result of the study.

Closing meditation

---

[3] Taken from a biography of William Carey by James Culross, available at <http://website.lineone.net/~gsward/pages/wcarey.html> (accessed 23 November 2008).

Week 6: Courtesy: 'Sorry!'

Opening activity and prayer

Talk together as a group about how and when you were taught manners – like saying please and thank you, not interrupting others, holding doors open, giving up your seat, not pushing into a queue. Some people complain that we are losing these values today. What are the most important manners to hang on to?

This final week we begin with a prayer of Jane Austen – a classic English novelist who showed 'tolerance and good manners' in her writing. We can pray it together as we begin.

Incline us, O God, to think humbly of ourselves, to be severe only in the examination of our own conduct, to consider our fellow-creatures with kindness, and to judge all they say and do with that charity which we would desire from them ourselves; through Jesus Christ our Lord. Amen.

Reflection

One of the strangest (and perhaps most beautiful) things about English people is that if someone bumps into us in the street we say 'sorry!' to them, even though it's they who have bumped into us. Kate Fox proves this over and over again by actually doing it. Once she has got over the reflex that leads her, too, to say sorry before the other person, she records 80 per cent of people as saying sorry – and the figure largely holds regardless of the other person's ethnic background or age. This does not happen in the same way in other countries when she tries it out.

There are also other times when we say sorry – for example, before we ask a stranger a question or when someone is in our way and we need them to move. Sometimes it must seem to outsiders that we might even be sorry that we exist at all!

So this week's saying is simply the word 'Sorry!' – and all the associated thoughts and feelings that go with it for us.

1 Creating a cultural world

Draw a circle in the middle of a flip-chart sheet and write 'Sorry!' in the middle of the circle. Then divide the sheet up into four parts from the centre. As before, we ask four sets of questions of this world of 'Sorry!'

2 Relating to the tradition

The group should take up to five minutes to generate passages from the Bible or other elements of the Christian tradition which resonate with 'Sorry!' It is best if a short extract or sentence is chosen which sums up the passage. These are listed on the flip chart. This final week I am not going to suggest any, because by now the group should be used to this stage of the reflection.

The group then should reflect together for a further five minutes on which passage best matches the saying 'Sorry!'

3 Creating a world from the tradition

Draw the four quadrants again and then ask similar questions to those above – but now of the world created by this new phrase, sentence or idea.

4 Comparing and contrasting the worlds

Once this flip chart is complete, place it alongside the one with 'Sorry!' at the centre. Now compare and contrast the four quadrants.

There are three more stages left, the first of which may be left out if there is little time remaining.

5 Telling our stories

6 Taking positions

Allow everyone five minutes in quiet to prepare a 'position statement', both from their own interaction with this week's reflection and for the course as whole. This week, then, we'll be sharing two positions – one relating to 'courtesy' and one expressing our final standpoint after all the reflections.

7 Taking action

Again, allow each person a few minutes to think what actions, if any, they might take, both as a result of this week's study and of the course as a whole.

8 Review of the course

Take some time to look back over the course. Or this could be left until the optional seventh week's session.

- What has been helpful?
- How have people changed?
- What connections have been made between our faith and English culture?
- Where are the disconnections?

Closing meditation

Optional week 7: Implications of what we have learnt

Rather than give a full outline for this final study, we simply offer some ideas here for the facilitator(s) to work with so that the course can be completed well.

1 If a review of the course has not been done yet, start with the general questions offered at the end of Week 6.
2 Now review in detail each of the sessions and ask what implications there might be from the insights gained for engaging with people who, when asked about their religion, call themselves Christians, but who never come to church. For instance, how can we use English humour in the service of the gospel? How can our homes be open places where community is built?
3 Think about the possibility of offering the course for 'Christian' people outside the Church through an adult education centre or equivalent.
4 Complete and present the English Christ meditations and the course findings to an invited group of guests.

Bibliography

Allen, John (2006), *Rabble-Rouser for Peace: The Authorized Biography of Desmond Tutu*, London: Random House

Arbuckle, Gerald A. (1990), *Earthing the Gospel: An Inculturation Handbook for the Pastoral Worker*, Maryknoll: Orbis

Astley, Jeff (1994), *The Philosophy of Christian Religious Education*, Birmingham, AL: Religious Education Press

Barnes, Julian (1998), *England, England*, London: Vintage

Bartholomew, Craig (2005), 'In Front of the Text: The Quest for Hermeneutics' in Ballard, Paul and Holmes, Stephen R., eds, *The Bible in Pastoral Practice: Readings in the Place and Function of Scripture in the Church*, London: DLT, pp. 135–52

Bediako, Kwame (1999), 'Translatability and the Cultural Incarnations of the Faith' in Scherer, James, A. and Bevans, Stephen B., eds, *New Directions in Mission and Evangelization 3: Faith and Culture*, Maryknoll: Orbis, pp. 146–58

Bediako, Kwame (2008), '"Why Has the Summer Ended and We Are Not Saved?" Encountering the Real Challenge of Christian Engagement in Primal Contexts', *Journal of African Christian Thought*, Vol. 11, No. 2, pp. 5–14

Bevans, Stephen B. (2002), *Models of Contextual Theology*, Revised and Expanded Edition, Maryknoll: Orbis

Bradley, Ian (2008), *Believing in Britain: The Spiritual Identity of Britishness*, Oxford: Lion

Bragg, Billy (2006), *The Progressive Patriot: A Search for Belonging*, London: Bantam Press

Brown, Callum G. (2001), *The Death of Christian Britain*, London: Routledge

Brueggemann, Walter (2005), 'The Re-emergence of Scripture: Post-liberalism' in Ballard, Paul and Holmes, Stephen R., eds, *The Bible in Pastoral Practice: Readings in the Place and Function of Scripture in the Church*, London: DLT, pp. 153–73

Bryson, Bill (1995), *Notes from a Small Island*, London: Doubleday

Clarke, Graham (1990), *Joe Carpenter & Son: An English Nativity*, Oxford: Phaidon

Clayton, Philip (1999), 'Missiology between Monologue and Cacophony' in Kirk, J. Andrew and Vanhoozer, Kevin J., eds, *To Stake a Claim: Mission and the Crisis of Western Knowledge*, Maryknoll: Orbis, pp. 78–95

Clifford, Sue and King, Angela (2006), *England in Particular: A Celebration of the Commonplace, the Local, the Vernacular and the Distinctive*, London: Hodder & Stoughton

The Cloud of Unknowing and Other Works (2001), trans. Spearing, A. C., London: Penguin

Cosgrove, Charles H. and Edgerton, W. Dow (2007), *In Other Words: Incarnational Translation for Preaching*, Grand Rapids, MI: Eerdmans

Davie, Grace (1994), *Religion in Britain Since 1945: Believing Without Belonging*, Oxford: Blackwell

Davie, Grace (2002), *Europe: The Exceptional Case: Parameters of Faith in the Modern World*, London: DLT

Donovan, Vincent J. (1978), *Christianity Rediscovered: An Epistle from the Masai*, SCM: London

Drane, John (2000), *The McDonaldization of the Church*, London: DLT

Drane, John (2005), *Do Christians Know How to Be Spiritual? The Rise of New Spirituality and the Mission of the Church*, London: DLT

Drane, John (2008), *After McDonaldization: Mission, Ministry and the Future of the Church*, London: DLT

Fox, Kate (2004), *Watching the English: The Hidden Rules of English Behaviour*, London: Hodder and Stoughton

Freire, Paulo (1972), *Pedagogy of the Oppressed*, Penguin: Harmondsworth

Gadamer, Hans-Georg (1989), *Truth and Method*, 2nd revised edn, translated by [1975] Weinsheimer, Joel and Marshall, Donald G., London: Sheed and Ward

Gittins, Anthony J. (1993), *Bread for the Journey: The Mission of Transformation and the Transformation of Mission*, Maryknoll: Orbis

Gittins, Anthony J. ed. (2000), *Life and Death Matters: The Practice of Inculturation in Africa*, Nettetal: Steyler Verlag

Gorringe, Timothy (2004), *Furthering Humanity: A Theology of Culture*, Aldershot: Ashgate

Gorski, John F. (2004), 'Christology, Inculturation and their Missiological Implications: A Latin American Perspective', *International Bulletin of Missionary Research*, Vol. 28, No. 2, pp. 60–3

Graham, Elaine, Walton, Heather and Ward, Frances (2005), *Theological Reflection: Methods*, London: SCM

Green, Laurie (1990), *Let's Do Theology: A Pastoral Cycle Resource Book*, London: Continuum

Groome, Thomas H. (1980), *Christian Religious Education: Sharing Our Story and Vision*, New York: Harper and Row

Habermas, Jürgen (1978), *Knowledge and Human Interests*, 2nd edn with appendix, translated by Shapiro, Jeremy J., London: Heinemann

Hastings, Adrian (1994), *The Church in Africa: 1450–1950*, Oxford: Clarendon Press

Hay, David and Hunt, Kate (2000), *Understanding the Spirituality of People Who Don't Go to Church*, Nottingham: Nottingham University

Healey, Joseph and Sybertz, Donald (1997), *Towards an African Narrative Theology*, Nairobi: Paulines Publications Africa

Heelas, Paul and Woodhead, Linda (eds) (2005), *The Spiritual Revolution: Why Religion Is Giving Way to Spirituality*, Oxford: Blackwell

Hiebert, Paul G. (2008), *Transforming Worldviews: An Anthropological Understanding of How People Change*, Grand Rapids, MI: Baker

Jasper, David (2004), *A Short Introduction to Hermeneutics*, Louisville, KY: Westminster John Knox Press

Johns, Cheryl B. (1993), *Pentecostal Formation: A Pedagogy Among the Oppressed*, Sheffield: Sheffield Academic Press

Jones, Edwin (2003), *The English Nation: The Great Myth*, Stroud: Sutton Publishing

Khorsandi, Shappi (2009), *A Beginner's Guide to Acting English*, London: Ebury Press

Killen, Patricia O'Connell and De Beer, John (1994), *The Art of Theological Reflection*, New York: Crossroad

Kingsnorth, Paul (2008), *Real England: The Battle Against the Bland*, London: Portobello Books

Knight, Stephen (2003), *Robin Hood: A Mythic Biography*, Ithaca/London: Cornell University Press

Kolb, David A. (1984), *Experiential Learning: Experience as the Source of Learning and Development*, Englewood Cliffs, NJ: Prentice Hall

Kraft, Charles H. (1996), *Anthropology for Christian Witness*, Maryknoll: Orbis

Lyall, Sarah (2008), *A Field Guide to the English*, London: Quercus

Magesa, Laurenti (2004), *Anatomy of Inculturation: Transforming the Church in Africa*, Maryknoll: Orbis

Mezirow, Jack and associates (1990), *Fostering Critical Reflection in Adulthood: A Guide to Transformative and Emancipatory Learning*, San Francisco: Jossey-Bass

Miles, David (2006), *The Tribes of Britain: Who Are We and Where Do We Come From?*, London: Orion

Mission and Public Affairs Council (MPAC), Church of England (2004), *Mission-Shaped Church: Church Planting and Fresh Expressions of Church in a Changing Context*, London: Church House Publishing

Moreton, Cole (2010), *Is God Still an Englishman? How We Lost Our Faith (But Found New Soul)*, London: Little, Brown

Mursell, Gordon (2001), *English Spirituality: From Earliest Times to 1700*, London: SPCK

Nagy, Joseph F. (1999), 'The Paradoxes of Robin Hood', in Knight, Stephen (ed.), *Robin Hood: Anthology of Scholarship and Criticism*, Cambridge: D. S. Brewer, pp. 411–25

Newbigin, Lesslie (1995), *Proper Confidence: Faith, Doubt and Certainty in Christian Discipleship*, Grand Rapids, MI: Eerdmans

Niebuhr, H. Richard (1951), *Christ and Culture*, New York: Harper and Row

Nussbaum, Stan (1998), *The ABCs of American Culture: Understanding the American People through their Common Sayings*, Colorado Springs: Global Mapping International

Paxman, Jeremy (1999), *The English: A Portrait of a People*, London: Penguin

Pollard, A. J. (2007), *Imagining Robin Hood: The Late-Medieval Stories in Historical Context*, Abingdon: Routledge

Ricoeur, Paul (1970), *Freud and Philosophy: An Essay on Interpretation*, trans. Savage, Denis, London: Yale University Press

Ricoeur, Paul (1981), *Hermeneutics and the Human Sciences: Essays on Language, Action and Interpretation*, ed. and trans. Thompson, John B., Cambridge: Cambridge University Press

Rooms, Nigel (2005), 'Inculturation Comes Home: Lessons from the Worldwide Church', *Anvil* Vol. 22, No. 4

Rooms, Nigel (2010), 'English and Christian? Negotiating Christian Cultural Identity Through Imaginative Theological Pedagogy', *Practical Theology* Vol. 3.1

Sanneh, Lamin (1989), *Translating the Message: The Missionary Impact on Culture*, Maryknoll: Orbis

Schön, Donald A. (1991), *The Reflective Practitioner: How Professionals Think in Action*, Aldershot: Ashgate

Schreiter, Robert J. (1985), *Constructing Local Theologies*, Maryknoll: Orbis

Schreiter, Robert J. (1997), *The New Catholicity: Theology Between the Global and the Local*, Maryknoll: Orbis

Sedmak, Clemens (2002), *Doing Local Theology: A Guide for Artisans of a New Humanity*, Maryknoll: Orbis

Sentamu, John (2009), 'England Rediscovered', edited text version of a speech given to the 2009 Sunday Times Oxford Literary Festival, *Third Way*, Vol. 32, No. 5

Smith, Mark K. (1999), 'Knowledge', web article at <www.infed.org/biblio/knowledge.htm>, accessed 20 April 2006

Spencer, Nick (ed.) (2010), 'Shaping a Nation: The Influence of the Bible on British Culture', *The Bible in Transmission: A Forum for Change in Church and Culture*, Swindon: Bible Society, Spring 2010

Syal, Meera (1997), *Anita and Me*, London: Flamingo

Thiselton, Anthony C. (1980), *The Two Horizons*, Grand Rapids, MI: Eerdmans

Thiselton, Anthony C. (1992), *New Horizons in Hermeneutics*, London: HarperCollins

Veling, Terry A. (2005), *Practical Theology: 'On Earth as it is in Heaven'*, Maryknoll: Orbis

Walls, Andrew F. (1999), 'The Gospel as Prisoner and Liberator of Culture', in Scherer, James, A. and Bevans, Stephen B., eds, *New Directions in Mission and Evangelization 3: Faith and Culture*, Maryknoll: Orbis, pp. 17–28

Walls, Andrew F. (2002), *The Cross-cultural Process in Christian History*, Maryknoll: Orbis

Wells, Samuel and Coakley, Sarah (eds) (2008), *Praying for England: Priestly Presence in Contemporary Culture*, London: Continuum

Williams, Peter (2009), 'Pragmatic, comfortable, unobtrusive: Can the Church of England ever learn to Evangelise?', *Anvil* Vol. 26, No. 2, pp. 123–45

Wood, Michael (2000), *In Search of England: Journeys into the English Past*, London: Penguin

Index